Freedom of Information Act

LANDMARK LEGISLATION

Freedom of
Information Act

Susan Dudley Gold

Marshall Cavendish
Benchmark
New York

Dedicated to investigative reporters everywhere, who devote their time and sometimes their lives to uncovering the truth.

With thanks to Catherine McGlone, Esq., for her expert review of this manuscript.

Copyright © 2012 Susan Dudley Gold
Published by Marshall Cavendish Benchmark
An imprint of Marshall Cavendish Corporation
All rights reserved.

This publication represents the opinions and views of Susan Dudley Gold based on her personal experience, knowledge, and research. The information in this book serves as a general guide only. The author and publisher have used their best efforts in preparing this book and disclaim liability rising directly and indirectly from the use and application of this book.

Other Marshall Cavendish Offices:
Marshall Cavendish International (Asia) Private Limited, 1 New Industrial Road, Singapore 536196 • Marshall Cavendish International (Thailand) Co. Ltd. 253 Asoke, 12th Flr, Sukhumvit 21 Road, Klongtoey Nua, Wattana, Bangkok 10110, Thailand • Marshall Cavendish (Malaysia) Sdn Bhd, Times Subang, Lot 46, Subang Hi-Tech Industrial Park, Batu Tiga, 40000 Shah Alam, Selangor Darul Ehsan, Malaysia
Marshall Cavendish is a trademark of Times Publishing Limited

All websites were available and accurate when this book was sent to press.

Library of Congress Cataloging-in-Publication Data
Gold, Susan Dudley.
Freedom of Information Act / by Susan Dudley Gold.
p. cm. -- (Landmark legislation)
Includes bibliographical references and index.
ISBN 978-1-60870-485-9 (Print) ISBN 978-1-60870-707-2 (eBook)
1. United States. Freedom of Information Act–Juvenile literature. 2. Government information–United States. 3. Freedom of information–United States--Juvenile literature. I. Title.
KF5753.G65 2012
342.7308'53--dc22
2010023504

Publisher: Michelle Bisson
Art Director: Anahid Hamparian
Series Designer: Sonia Chaghatzbanian
Photo research by Custom Communications Inc.

Cover photo: Oliver North holds up a classified document during congressional hearings on the Iran-Contra affair.

The photographs in this book are used by permission and through the courtesy of: *AP Images*: 6, 27, 32, 37; Lana Harris, cover; Krista Niles, 3, 91; Dan Grossi, 44; Byron Rollins, 74; Joe Marquette, 81; Alex Brandon, 115; *Getty Images*: David Fenton, 48; Ralph Crane/ Time Life Pictures, 59; AFP, 89; Brad Markel, 97; Tom Williams/Roll Call, 103; *Lyndon Baines Johnson Library*: 71, 79; *John E. Moss Foundation*: 85; *North Wind Picture Archives*: 14, 16, 19; *Zuma Press*: Tami Silicio, 2, 31.

Contents

U.S. Representative John Moss, chairman of the House Subcommittee on Government Information, holds a sheaf of papers marked "secret" on May 4, 1961, to illustrate the overuse of the classification system to keep government documents hidden from Americans. Moss fought a twelve-year campaign to pass the Freedom of Information Act and open government records to the public.

A Citizen's Right to Information

The power of information can destroy corrupt public officials, bankrupt ruthless companies, and shut down the illegal operations of federal agencies. It can prevent illness in millions of people, save countless others from injury, and keep federal officials in line. The American democratic system—a government of the people, by the people, and for the people—depends on its citizens to hold government accountable. But until 1966, when Congress passed the Freedom of Information Act (FOIA), there was no law on the books that required officials to respond in a systematic way to citizens' requests for government records.

The Freedom of Information Act gives Americans access to the ammunition they need—information—to fight city hall and corporate wrongdoing. It gives citizens, journalists, and public interest groups a way to check on how government agencies spend taxpayers' money, whether officials perform their jobs efficiently and appropriately, and how they arrive at the decisions they make. People have also used the FOIA to track down long-lost relatives, check on a spouse's assets during divorce proceedings, and look for evidence of UFO landings.

In a development that might surprise the FOIA's authors, businesses have become the biggest users of the law today. They rely on the FOIA to obtain government data on their industry, information about competitors and clients, and documents related to private business matters.

The FOIA acknowledges that government has good reasons to withhold certain information from the public. Under the law, officials can keep documents secret to protect national security. They can also withhold private information (such as medical or other records), trade secrets, and confidential commercial and financial information, some law enforcement records, confidential bank records, certain letters and memos at federal agencies, and documents sealed by court order.

The Freedom of Information Act was necessary because the U.S. Constitution contains no guarantee of a citizen's right to knowledge about the government. Under the Constitution, Congress is required to publish a record of its proceedings, except for portions that the members determine need to be kept secret. There is no similar constitutional requirement for the president or the agencies and departments under the administration's control. The Freedom of Information Act applies only to the federal agencies and departments in the executive branch of government. It does not apply to Congress, to the courts, or to the president.

Anyone can apply to review government documents under the FOIA. People petitioning under the FOIA do not have to say why they need the materials or present evidence that the information should come to light. If the government does not turn over the requested materials, the FOIA gives citizens and others the right to sue in federal court to gain access. Under the law, the government has to prove that documents should remain hidden. Information can only be withheld if it falls within one of nine exemptions, including national security.

The law came about because of the determination of a young congressman from California who made it his mission to open government records to the public. John E. Moss directed the effort from his Subcommittee on Government Information, which he chaired and from which he conducted hearings into government secrecy. His campaign met with instant opposition from many quarters: members of Congress, presidents, and the departments and agencies within the executive branch, including the armed forces, law enforcement agencies, and every member of the Cabinet.

Commentator Bill Moyers, who served as President Lyndon Johnson's press secretary at the time of the law's enactment, gives Moss full credit for the legislation. "Only the courage and political skill of a Congressman named John Moss got the bill passed at all," said Moyers, "and that was after a twelve-year battle against his elders in Congress who blinked every time the sun shined in the dark corridors of power."

The law, and the subsequent amendments that tightened some of the loopholes, has led to the release of millions of pages of government records. Some of those documents have helped force corrupt politicians from office, brought about changes in government policy, and applied pressure for safer products. Among the changes FOIA helped initiate:

- Citizens in 1978 forced Ford Motor Company to recall the Pinto, a subcompact car with a gas tank that had a tendency to explode on impact. The FOIA documents showed that Ford had known about the gas tank defect but had produced it anyway because it was cheaper than installing a safer tank.

• The Federal Drug Administration banned the use of Red No. 2 dye in food products in 1977 after winning its FOIA lawsuit to release information on the substance. The data linked the dye to cancer.

• The disclosure of wrongdoing in more than 2,500 pages of documents released under the FOIA led to the resignation of Vice President Spiro Agnew in 1973. The material gathered under the FOIA revealed evidence of bribery, extortion, and other criminal behavior by Agnew.

• The years-long battle by the American Civil Liberties Union (ACLU) to unearth reports on the military's treatment of prisoners after September 11, 2001, produced a mountain of documents on the torture and abuse meted out by U.S. soldiers at secret overseas jails. The ensuing public outcry persuaded Congress to address the issue, led to the release of several prisoners who had no charges against them, and caused President Barack Obama to sign executive orders barring the use of torture of enemy soldiers.

When Congress passed the Freedom of Information Act on June 20, 1966, Senator Edward V. Long, a Missouri Democrat who sponsored the bill in the Senate, called its passage "a historic victory for the public's constitutional right to know what their government is doing."

CHAPTER ONE

Keeping Secrets

Officials in early America cloaked
their activities in secrecy and struggled to keep their actions
secret at all costs. Early journalists worked equally hard to
reveal official secrets. The colonists carried printing presses
from Europe to their new homes in America, along with a
strong distaste for government censorship. The colonies'
first newspaper, *Publick Occurrences Both Forreign and
Domestick*, published only one edition—a blistering attack
on Boston's colonial officials. On September 25, 1690, the
day the article appeared, the Massachusetts colonial government shut down the newspaper, arrested its publisher, and
destroyed every copy it could find.

The *Boston News-Letter* became the first newspaper to
publish on a regular basis in North America. Its first edition, published on April 24, 1704, and those that followed
reported on English politics, the progress of European wars,
shipping news, deaths, and other items of interest to local

readers. The newspaper, published by postmaster John Campbell and subsidized by the colonial government, stayed in business by avoiding criticism of colonial officials. The *Boston Gazette*, first published in 1719, followed a similar course of not reporting unfavorably on local politicians. England kept a tight rein on its British colonies in America, and in particular, on colonial publishers. "Great inconvenience may arise by the liberty of printing," British agents warned government officers in charge of Massachusetts in the seventeenth century. The British government required all colonial printers to obtain a license to operate. Local officials could revoke the license at their discretion and imprison printers who continued to publish.

Nevertheless, colonial firebrands found ways to get their reports of government doings in print. They circulated flyers and pamphlets attacking government policies and actions. The agents of the British Crown in Massachusetts tried to stop these reports by requiring printers to obtain official permission before printing anything. The Massachusetts assembly members voted against the proposal, saying that the policy would create "innumerable inconveniences and danger" for colonists. Massachusetts legislators rejected a similar bill that would have barred libelous material from being published, with punishment for those who disobeyed the prohibition. That defeat ended English efforts to control printing presses in Massachusetts, but local legislators enacted their own laws. In 1725 the Massachusetts legislature made it illegal for newspapers to report on the meetings of local government officials. The debate got heated at times, and lawmakers feared that the British king might retaliate after reading an angry critic's words in the newspaper.

The tension between newspapers and officials increased

as the number of newspapers grew in the colonies. In 1733 government officials threw John Peter Zenger in jail after his *New York Weekly Journal* published reports critical of the colonial governor. At his trial on charges of libel, Zenger claimed as his defense that the newspaper reports were true and that the truth should not be considered libel. The jury agreed with Zenger, and the case became a landmark for a free press in America.

By the 1770s, two dozen or so newspapers published regular editions, mostly in the colonies of the Northeast. During the years leading up to the American Revolution, flyers and underground newspapers played a vital part in keeping citizens informed of official misconduct and spreading discontent with British rule. Thomas Paine's pamphlet, *Common Sense*, made the case for independence and helped ignite the spark of revolution in America. "No pamphlet, no book, ever kindled such a sudden conflagration," said noted nineteenth-century orator Robert G. Ingersoll of Paine's treatise.

By the end of the war, more than forty newspapers carried reports of events to the citizenry. As important as printed materials had been in stirring up the revolution, newspapers now played a key role in a new nation: protecting its people from abuse of power. The new system of government—a democracy—depended on informed citizens to raise the alarm against tyrants.

Delegates to the Constitutional Convention met in 1787 to form the new government and write a constitution based on rule by the people. Ironically, the delegates debated and voted on these monumental decisions in secret. James Madison, who later served as America's third president and was an ardent supporter of openness in government, nevertheless believed that the proceedings should be kept secret. He wrote

British soldiers burned John Peter Zenger's printing press in New York in 1733 after he published reports critical of the colonial governor.

U.S. Constitution

extensive notes of the sessions, during which the nation's leaders framed the U.S. Constitution. But he stipulated that the notes should not be released during his lifetime. They were eventually published in 1840, four years after Madison's death. Many agreed with Madison that if the discussions had been published immediately after the convention, Americans would never have ratified the Constitution. "The dialogue contained far too much that would have been seized upon by demagogues," observed Irving Brant, a former news reporter and editor who became Madison's biographer.

The secrecy surrounding the convention did not sit well with Thomas Jefferson, for one. In an angry letter to John Adams in 1787, Jefferson proclaimed the importance of holding the discussions in public. "I am sorry they began their deliberations by so abominable a precedent as that of tying up the tongues of their members," he wrote. Adams, long a champion of open government, had earlier addressed

George Washington presides over the Constitutional Convention in 1787.

the secrecy issue, in 1765 in his essay on law: "Liberty," he wrote, "cannot be preserved without a general knowledge among the people, who have a right . . . to knowledge; but besides this, they have a right, an indisputable, unalienable, indefeasible, divine right to that most dreaded and envied kind of knowledge; I mean, of the characters and conduct of their rulers." Neither Adams nor Jefferson attended the secret sessions of the Constitutional Convention.

Madison, who helped write the final version of the U.S. Constitution, would later become a chief spokesman for openness in government. "A popular Government, without popular information, or the means of acquiring it, is but a Prologue to a Farce or a Tragedy; or, perhaps both. Knowledge will forever govern ignorance: And a people who mean to be their own Governors, must arm themselves with the power which knowledge gives," Madison wrote in an 1822 letter to W. T. Barry, a Kentucky lawyer who served in both the U.S. House of Representatives and the U.S. Senate.

The Constitution itself contains no guarantee of a citizen's right to know. James Wilson, the representative from Pennsylvania at the constitutional convention, spoke in favor of adding a clause requiring a public record of Congress's actions and debates. "The people have a right to know what their agents are doing or have done, and it should not be in the option of the legislature to conceal their proceedings," he said. Instead, the founders included a requirement in the Constitution that Congress publish "from time to time" a record of its proceedings, along with a record of votes taken. The members of the House and Senate can decide, however, to keep certain information secret.

A "DARK VEIL OF SECRECY"

During the ratification of the Constitution, several state leaders lobbied for a tougher requirement for open government. Patrick Henry, for one, argued that the Constitution should include a specific deadline for Congress to publish its proceedings. The phrase "from time to time" had "more than once" allowed activities to take place "under the dark veil of secrecy," Henry stated. "The liberties of a people never were nor ever will be secure, when the transactions of their rulers may be concealed from them."

The states ratified the Constitution as proposed, without a stronger open-government clause. As part of a compromise to convince states to ratify the federal Constitution, the framers subsequently wrote ten amendments that guaranteed rights to citizens and individual states. These are known as the Bill of Rights. Madison wrote the First Amendment, which focuses on free speech and expression, freedom of religion,

George Washington's Secrets

As the nation's first president, George Washington set many precedents, including keeping secrets. He oversaw a stash of money known as the Secret Service Fund, which by 1793 held more than $1 million (about 12 percent of the national budget). The money funded foreign intelligence operations and America's dealings with other countries. Congress, which allocated the money for the fund, required the president to report how much he spent, but Washington did not have to reveal why he doled out the money or who received it.

Washington first claimed executive privilege to hide military information from Congress. The showdown between Washington and Congress came during the president's first term when the House of Representatives launched an investigation into the army's devastating loss to Native Americans in the Northwest Territory.

In 1791 Washington sent General Arthur St. Clair to lead an attack against the tribes, who had joined forces under Tecumseh, a young Shawnee warrior. In a surprise attack, the Native Americans wiped out almost the entire army under St. Clair's command. The rout remains the worst defeat in the army's history. When Congress subpoenaed the records of the battle, Washington asked the members of his Cabinet for their advice on the matter. The Cabinet members determined that the separation of powers under the U.S. Constitution gave the executive branch and the legislative branch equal weight. That meant that Congress did not have the power to order the president to release the documents. In the end, Washington allowed Congress to see the records, but the incident cemented the concept of executive privilege for all future presidents.

Washington invoked executive privilege again in a dispute

President Washington's first Cabinet, from left, Henry Knox, Thomas Jefferson, Alexander Hamilton, and Edmund Randolph. The man with his back to the viewer is unidentified.

over the Jay Treaty. In 1795 he ordered John Jay to go to London to negotiate a settlement with Britain to end hostilities between the two nations. Neither the public nor the House of Representatives nor the president's opponents in the Senate knew of the mission. After the Senate approved Jay's deal, the House demanded that Washington turn over all the papers concerning the treaty. He refused to comply and thus reaffirmed the power of the president to keep secrets from Congress and the public.

From Washington's day to the twenty-first century, presidents have maintained their right as head of the executive branch to keep certain records secret. Often in such battles with Congress, the two sides work out a compromise that allows members of Congress access to at least some of the materials they need but maintains the president's right to retain the power of executive privilege.

and freedom of the press. The founders saw these freedoms as essential to a democracy. They protected the press as a valuable tool to keep the American people informed about their government.

Debates, reports, and a record of proceedings of both houses of Congress can be viewed in the *Annals of Congress* for the years 1789 to 1824. The publisher, the Gales and Seaton Company, collected newspaper reports and summaries of debates and proceedings in the early years of Congress and published the annals beginning in 1834. The *Register of Debates*, published each session from 1824 to 1837, covered congressional debates and actions for those years. The *Congressional Globe* produced a similar report on Congress's sessions from 1833 to 1873. In 1873 Congress itself began printing a daily report of its activities. These are collected in the *Congressional Record*, which continues to provide a comprehensive report on Congress's activities during each session.

These records, however, do not necessarily ensure that the American people know what the federal government is doing. Through the years Congress has prevented the release of information in a number of ways. One method was to pass laws that barred the release or publication of certain types of information. Included in such bans were articles, speeches, and reports critical of the government or government officials, or any material related to the defense of the nation. Congress frequently passed these laws in times of war or peril. In many cases, but not all, the U.S. Supreme Court has ultimately ruled laws unconstitutional that tried to limit speech critical of the government. The Court has upheld laws and regulations that have prevented access to military secrets and other information related to national security.

Not long after the ratification of the First Amendment,

Congress passed a law that provided legal backing for those in the government who wanted to control information. The Alien and Sedition Acts of 1798 made it a crime to print "false, scandalous and malicious writing" about the government, Congress, or the president. Those convicted of violating the new law faced fines of up to $5,000 (more than $100,000 in today's dollars) and up to five years in prison. Congress enacted the law during an undeclared war with France after that nation seized U.S. naval ships and personnel. Supporters of the law claimed that it was necessary to protect the nation from threats from France. They also hoped to use the law against Thomas Jefferson and his supporters.

Matthew Lyon, a U.S. representative from Vermont, was the first to be arrested under the law. Lyon, a Jefferson supporter, had written a letter to the editor opposing war with France and accusing President John Adams of being "swallowed up in a continued grasp of power." The jury, filled with Adams supporters, found Lyon guilty of writing with "bad intent," and the judge, also pro–Adams, sentenced the congressman to four months in prison and fined him $1,000. Lyon's constituents reelected him while he served out his sentence in a Vermont jail. The public outrage over Lyon's sentence helped elect Jefferson as president in 1800. Once in office, Jefferson issued pardons to those convicted under the Alien and Sedition Acts. In 1801 Congress allowed the law to expire and reimbursed fees plus interest to everyone who had paid a fine under the acts.

Threats of another war led to a second sedition act, this one passed in 1918 as an amendment to the Espionage Act of 1917. Among other things, it prohibited "profane, scurrilous, or abusive language" about the government, the Constitution, or the army and navy. Congress repealed the act in

1921, but not before more than two thousand citizens were prosecuted and dozens of books, newspapers, and journals were banned under its provisions. Socialist Eugene V. Debs received a ten-year jail sentence after being convicted of violating the law for speaking publicly against World War I.

The USA Patriot Act, which called for a number of measures to keep information secret, won almost unanimous support from Congress in 2001. It was enacted shortly after terrorist attacks on the World Trade Center in New York City and the Pentagon on September 11. U.S. agencies, including the CIA, used the law to conduct secret counterterrorism operations that have come under fire, including torturing suspects and detaining them without access to lawyers. Although the act includes provisions that require officials to report to Congress, President George W. Bush disputed that stipulation when he signed the bill in 2001. In a statement submitted with his copy of the bill, Bush declared that only the executive branch (the president and his departments, including the Justice Department) had the power to determine which information it would share with Congress or the public. The Patriot Act continues in force in 2011. Congress and President Barack Obama, who took office in 2009, ordered an end to several operations, however, including torture and secret detentions, after press reports brought the practices to light.

CONTROLLED, CLASSIFIED, AND OUT OF REACH

Congress passed the first regulations on handling government documents in 1787. With the formation of a strong federal government came the need to organize the work of the various federal agencies. President George Washington asked Congress to pass a law that authorized members of his Cabinet to set up their own ways of handling their agencies' documents. Congress enacted the so-called Housekeeping Act in 1787. It put department heads in charge of providing for the "custody, use and preservation" of the documents within their agencies. This resulted in a hodgepodge of rules and practices for the handling of government documents. For the most part, the early government agencies made information available to those who requested it.

Critics of secrecy contend that Washington—and Congress—never intended the Housekeeping Act to be used as a tool to hide official documents from the public. Nevertheless, the law gave agency heads the power to bury records they wanted to keep secret. Through the years federal agencies developed an elaborate classification system of government documents that allowed officials to keep sensitive information hidden. Officials thought these measures were necessary to protect the nation's security as well as to safeguard private, personal information provided by citizens and businesses. But the system also made it easier for unscrupulous officials to hide documents that did not threaten national security, but revealed corruption or incompetence that would embarrass (or in some cases result in the arrest of) agency officials.

During the administration of Franklin D. Roosevelt the number of federal agencies increased dramatically. In 1946 Congress passed the Administrative Procedure Act (APA) to help standardize procedures at the agencies. One of the act's provisions established a uniform method for agencies to follow when distributing documents and other information. In approving the act, the House Judiciary Committee at the time noted that the law had been based on the "theory that administrative operations and procedures are public property which the general public, rather than a few specialists or lobbyists, is entitled to know."

Although the act stated support for the public's right to know, the APA in fact helped cement shut those records the government did not want circulated. Attorney General Tom Clark, in the manual he prepared on the APA in 1947, stated that one basic purpose of the APA was to "require agencies to keep the public currently informed of their organization, procedures and rules." Section Three of the law set up procedures designed to "assist the public in dealing with administrative agencies by requiring agencies to make their administrative materials available in precise and current form." However, big loopholes in Section Three allowed officials to withhold practically any document they wished to. Under the law, officials could refuse to disclose information involving "any function of the United States requiring secrecy in the public interest" and "any matter relating solely to the internal management of an agency." The law exempted "confidential operations" of all U.S. agencies.

Clark stated that materials should be kept from view only when they required "secrecy in the public interest." But he did not define the term, and he put agencies in charge of determining when information fell into that category. Further, the manual erected a wall of secrecy around military and foreign affairs. Accordingly, the APA rules on open access did not apply to any documents involving "a military or foreign affairs function of the United States." In addition, officials could withhold information merely by stating that they had "good cause" to keep the documents confidential. Such restrictions interfered not only with the public's access but also with Congress's ability to obtain information from federal agencies.

Another stumbling block was the APA's requirement that anyone wanting to examine a public document had to be "properly and directly concerned" with the materials. That meant that citizens, including members of the press, could not examine government paperwork unless they personally had a stake in the issue.

Federal officials used both the APA and the Housekeeping Act to withhold documents. Agencies routinely blocked the release of information unrelated to national security. The Atomic Energy Committee, for one, saw no reason to comply with the new law's aim to open government records. In a memo dated April 17, 1947, the agency expressed its policy on withholding records that might be embarrassing or otherwise reflect badly on the agency, a policy that many other agencies also followed: "It is desired that no document be released which . . . might have an adverse effect on public opinion or resulting legal suits."

Senators working to open government files concluded later that many officials used the APA "as an excuse for secrecy" and withheld documents "only to cover up embarrassing mistakes or irregularities." The law, the senators noted, had produced "widespread public dissatisfaction and confusion." In particular, the exemption granted to documents which required "secrecy in the public interest" had "in many cases . . . defeat[ed] the very purpose for which [the law] was intended—the public's right to know the operations of its Government." The result, they declared, was that the APA had become "an excuse for withholding" information rather than the "disclosure statute" it was intended to be.

Members of the public could do little to overcome refusals to produce documents: the APA contained no provisions to force agencies to comply and no punishment if they did not. The law also contained no provision for citizens to appeal a decision to withhold records.

After World War II, the cold war brought fears of Russian spies and put a chill on public access to government records. In 1946 the Atomic Energy Act automatically put some government information out of reach without officials ever having to classify it. The following year Congress passed the National Security Act, creating the Central Intelligence Agency and the National Security Council. The law also joined the branches of the armed forces under one agency, the Defense Department. A vast bureaucracy formed around these organizations, with secrecy as their lifeblood.

LOCKED BEHIND EXECUTIVE PRIVILEGE

The Constitution provides for a balance of power among the three branches of government: Congress as a representative of the people (legislative), the president and the departments serving under his or her administration (executive), and the courts (judicial). As equal partners, the branches share power; no one branch can rule over the others. As a separate and equal branch of government, presidents routinely claim their "executive privilege" to withhold information from Congress (maintaining that Congress cannot tell them what to do). Executive privilege serves a vital role in government by ensuring that presidential aides and advisers can speak openly without worrying that their words will be misconstrued by the press or critics outside the administration. Protecting the confidentiality of advisers allows a free flow of information, providing presidents with information and opinions they rely on to make decisions. Without such confidentiality, advisers might not explore topics that could be embarrassing or cast the administration in a negative light.

Executive privilege can interfere with the nation's democratic form of government, however, when presidents abuse

Washington Post reporters Carl Bernstein (*left*) and Robert Woodward uncovered the Watergate scandal that led to President Richard M. Nixon's resignation. They are pictured in 1973 after the *Post* won the Pulitzer Prize for public service for its reporting on the Watergate affair.

the power to keep secrets that citizens and Congress need to know. Congress cannot pass laws to correct a problem if a president, claiming executive privilege, hides information about that problem or if the pertinent facts about the problem are kept secret. That upsets the balance of power and limits Congress's ability to serve as the people's watchdog over a too-powerful chief executive.

The Watergate scandal that erupted during the term of President Richard M. Nixon centered around executive privilege. Nixon claimed the privilege to keep Congress from obtaining tapes of his conversations in the White House. The tapes, which the Supreme Court eventually ordered Nixon to release, revealed a conspiracy between the president and his aides to cover up fraud, a break-in at the Watergate complex, laundered money, and other illicit activities conducted during the 1972 presidential campaign.

In the 1980s members of President Ronald Reagan's administration arranged for weapons to be delivered to Iran in return for help in winning the release of seven U.S. hostages being held by Iranians in Lebanon. The deal took place during a U.S. ban on selling guns to Iran. In addition, some of the money from the arms sale went to support a rebel group in Nicaragua known as the Contras—all without the knowledge of Congress. A Lebanese newspaper exposed the guns-for-hostage deal in 1986, and Oliver North, who worked for the National Security Council, later testified on the affair during congressional hearings. No evidence linked Reagan to the deal, but fourteen members of his administration, including the secretary of defense, were indicted and eleven were convicted. The charges against North were eventually dismissed in exchange for his testimony.

A more recent use of executive privilege involved congressional charges that President George W. Bush had fired federal prosecutors for political gain. When Congress ordered two Bush aides to testify and to turn over documents relating to the matter, the president claimed executive privilege, ordered his aides not to appear, and refused to produce the papers in the case. Congress took the matter to court, but after appeals and delays, the case remained unresolved when Bush left office in 2009.

Courts are usually hesitant to decide disputes between Congress and a president over the release of information. Often the dispute involves political issues, and courts typically avoid contests between the branches of government. Congress has other tools at its disposal. Both the courts and Congress can issue subpoenas to demand the release of information from a president or agencies in the executive branch. If the information still is not delivered, a compromise may be negotiated. Congress may decrease the number of documents requested or limit the number of people who will view them. The public may apply pressure on a reluctant president or agency to turn over documents. In some cases, Congress may threaten to reduce the amount of money it allocates to an agency's programs as a tool to obtain information.

Because the Constitution provides for a system that balances power among the three branches of government, Congress has passed no law (including the FOIA) that gives its members the power to extract information from other branches. Congress often does not apply laws to its own proceedings. In the case of the FOIA, Congress reserved the right to make its own determinations whether certain information should remain secret. Congressional debates are open to the public and are recorded in the *Congressional Record*.

At times the press abides by an informal executive privilege by not publishing information on military or other operations the president wants withheld. Reporters and editors base these decisions on the notion that the information, if reported, might harm the nation or interfere with a military maneuver. In certain cases, premature reports would indeed interfere with a military operation and harm innocent victims. U.S. and Canadian journalists learned that Canadian diplomats were hiding six Americans after Iranian radicals stormed the U.S. embassy in Iran in 1979 and took the staff hostage. The media released the story of the six escapees only after they had returned home safely. More than fifty other Americans spent 444 days in captivity in Iran before being released. Jean Pelletier, reporter for the Quebec newspaper *La Presse*, the first journalist to learn of the hidden

Americans, persuaded his editor and publisher to hold the story. "You can't just simply apply your principle of publish-and-be-damned to each and every situation regardless of circumstance," Pelletier said in making his case to the paper's editor. Other newspapers, including the *New York Times*, also delayed publication of the story.

In some cases, however, critics contend that the press does more harm than good by keeping the public uninformed. During the George W. Bush administration, members of the press were "embedded" or allowed to accompany troops into battle in Iraq. The photographers on these missions refrained from broadcasting images of wounded and dying soldiers or of Iraqi villagers injured in U.S. attacks (although U.S. media had no similar ban on showing Iraqis killed in attacks by militant Islamist groups). Most media outlets also followed without protest the Bush administration's order not to photograph the coffins of dead soldiers returning to the United States.

By protecting Americans from war's brutality, critics say, the press helped glorify the war and tacitly supported U.S. actions without giving a balanced report on the true situation. The ban on showing dead or injured U.S. soldiers helped reinforce the message that America was winning the war and ignored the loss of American lives, the critics say. "Photos of American suffering or suffering caused by Americans might indeed sicken and offend viewers," writes Pat Arnow, photographer and former magazine editor. "But by acquiescing to the military's censorship and avoiding most of these images of American involvement, the media does not offer a true portrayal of the consequences of war." Graphic images of villagers wounded in U.S. attacks on Vietnam stirred up public protest against that war among Americans in the 1960s.

Tami Silicio and her husband, David Landry, lost their jobs with Maytag Aircraft, a military contractor in Kuwait, after the *Seattle Times* printed her photograph of flag-draped coffins of U.S. soldiers killed during the war in Iraq. The photograph was taken April 7, 2004, aboard a cargo plane at Kuwait International Airport. The Pentagon had banned such photographs since the Persian Gulf War in 1991, claiming they harmed the U.S. war effort. Defense Secretary Robert Gates lifted the ban in February 2009, as long as permission is obtained from the soldiers' families.

In defending their right to publish, members of the press note that citizens often have no other way of learning the truth about what their government is doing. Kent Cooper, executive director of the Associated Press, became the first to coin the phrase, "the people's right to know." In 1946 he lobbied for open government, arguing that neither the government nor the news media should "by any method whatever, curb delivery of any information essential to the public welfare and enlightenment."

Senator Joseph McCarthy (*center*) waves a transcript of a taped telephone call between G. David Schine (*left*) and Secretary of the Army Robert T. Stevens during a June 7, 1954, hearing of the Senate Permanent Subcommittee on Investigations. Roy M. Cohn, the committee's chief counsel, sits at right. McCarthy used the subcommittee to investigate the infiltration of communist subversives in the U.S. Army. The Wisconsin senator's unsubstantiated charges fanned fear of a communist takeover among the American public.

CHAPTER TWO

"A First, Timid Step"

The real origins of the campaign for public access to government documents began with Harold Cross and members of the American Society of Newspaper Editors (ASNE). Their main weapon, it turned out, was a book. The organization, founded in 1922, began its efforts in 1949 with the establishment of the Freedom of Information Committee. For several years the committee tried to persuade Congress to change government policy and open records to the public. When the committee made little progress, ASNE hired Cross, a retired journalism professor, to write a report on the "rights of newspapers and the various legal restrictions on their activities." Cross worked with the Freedom of Information Committee to compile a list of laws and court rulings that kept information secret. In 1953 Cross expanded the report into a book on the subject, *The People's Right to Know*.

Access to public records, Cross wrote in his book, served as a newspaper's "most vital raw material source." To do their job, newspapers had to be able to view public records and proceedings and report on the behavior, and sometimes misbehavior, of public officials. They also needed access to government records in order to explain policies, programs, and procedures, and the facts, discussions, and decisions that officials used in developing and approving them. "The right to speak and the right to print, without the right to know, are pretty empty," Cross noted.

In studying the problem of public access to records, Cross encountered a "welter of varying statutes, conflicting court decisions and wordy departmental regulations . . . a veritable Chinese puzzle." The jumble of laws included Florida's statute, which declared that "all state, county and municipal records" should "at all times be open for a personal inspection of any citizen." The law did not, however, define the term "records," which the courts interpreted in different ways, including the opinion that some documents could not be open to the public. Another law, in New Jersey, defined "public records" but did not require that they be opened to the public. Other states had no laws on public access at all. Without the guidance of clear, uniform laws, the state courts issued a wide variety of opinions on the matter.

Cross noted that current laws did much to hide public records from view and little to make them available to the press or the public. However, enterprising reporters often succeeded in gathering information either through contacts among staff members or by threatening unfavorable publicity if records were not released. Officials themselves sometimes made documents public to win support for their agency or program.

The first regulations, based on English common law, focused on the rights and privileges of the king. During the nation's early history, only a small number of government offices existed, few meddled in the affairs of citizens, and even fewer kept voluminous stacks of records. With the explosion of government agencies that began in the 1930s after the Great Depression, the small stack of records grew into a mountain of paperwork—much of which affected citizens' lives.

Under the 1787 Housekeeping Act, an agency director alone made the decision whether or not to release information under agency control. That meant that an agency director could decide whether to release the amount paid to federal employees, the terms of competitive bids for agency work, and a myriad of other details of interest to taxpayers. Cross reported that the Board of Engineers for Rivers and Harbors, for one, would not reveal how its board voted on the issues it decided. Another secret keeper, the State Department's Board of Review, refused to spell out the rules it followed when depriving a person of citizenship.

Recent laws and regulations, Cross wrote, had closed the books on financial dealings and judicial proceedings, particularly those involving families and juveniles. "The records are secret, period," he wrote. "Except for administrative officials or others specifically authorized, no one may inspect them."

Cross blamed the increasing tendency toward secrecy on six different trends:

- Governments throughout the world kept their operations secret.
- Officials fell into the habit of keeping secrets during wartime and continued to follow such policies after hostilities had ended.
- Right-to-privacy claims made it harder to obtain access to vital statistics and other official records.

- Proponents of secrecy, including social workers and welfare agents, successfully lobbied for laws that barred access to public records.
- Many people no longer believed that publicity served as a deterrent to crime, family abuse, irresponsible actions, or official wrongdoing.
- The press accepted the situation and did not fight for the right to view government records.

Cross concluded his treatise with a warning against "an official cult of secrecy." The executive branch, from the president to department heads to agency directors, would continue to bury their secrets until Congress corrected the abuses, Cross said. "In a democracy," he wrote, "such a state of affairs is a continuing challenge to public and press. Its growth has gone unchallenged too long." He urged Congress to use its power to enact a national law to protect the freedom of information and to make government records available. "The time is ripe for an end to ineffectual sputtering about executive refusals of access to official records and for Congress to . . . legislate freedom of information for itself, the public, and the press."

Cross's book served as a call to action for the nation's newspaper editors. ASNE's officers presented the first copy of the book to President Dwight D. Eisenhower. The book also caught the attention of a young Democratic congressman from California, John E. Moss. Early in his first term of office, Moss had objected to the Eisenhower administration's firing of hundreds of federal employees on the grounds that they were communists. Moss, believing there were other reasons behind the firings, asked the Civil Service Commission for paperwork that showed the cause of each dismissal. The commission brushed off his request. The freshman legislator soon learned there was nothing he could do to force the commission to show him the documents. As a result, Moss vowed to do something to pry open government records.

In 1955, after the release of the Cross report and book, Moss persuaded Congress to form a subcommittee to investigate government secrecy. Democrats had taken over control of Congress in the 1954 elections, and Moss's colleagues in the House allowed him to chair the three-member body, called the Special Subcommittee on Government Information.

COMMITTEE TESTIMONY

During hearings held by Moss's subcommittee in November 1955, several journalists testified that the government routinely withheld news and "managed" information in a way that distorted government policies. James S. Pope of Louisville, Kentucky's *The Courier-Journal* and the former head of ASNE's Freedom of Information Committee told Congress that federal agencies had "invaded and flouted" the public's right to have access to government records. He cited the Defense Department as the worst offender. "There is a state of mind of arrogance and contempt for the public on the part of some officials of the Government," Pope said. "The fact that we have to fight for freedom of information is a disgrace."

In further testimony, *Washington Post* executive editor J. Russell Wiggins warned of the "ominous" secrecy surrounding the Defense Department and the National Security Council. Newspaper editors, he noted, understood the need for military secrets in defense of the nation. But, he said, "they do not think that we need to make the hard choice between abandoning our safety and abandoning our freedom. They think we can have both safety and freedom."

John E. Moss:

From early childhood, John E. Moss learned to face challenges and not back down. Born in 1915, Moss lived in a poor coal-mining town in Utah. His family later moved to California, partly because young John had asthma and other health problems. Both his mother and his sister died when he was twelve, and his father abandoned Moss and his older brother, leaving them to care for themselves. The two young boys lived in a loft and worked odd jobs to support themselves. Dinner was often a cold can of spaghetti. Moss attended college for two years but could not continue because of lack of money. He later sold appliances and worked as a real estate broker. People who had never heard him argue a point would have described him as a mild-mannered, bespectacled, not-very-exciting businessman.

As a young man, Moss was president of the Sacramento Young Democrats and won election to the state assembly. He revered President Franklin D. Roosevelt as a hero of the nation's working people and adopted his role model's political values. In 1952 Moss won a tight election to represent the state in the U.S. House of Representatives. Almost as soon as he arrived, Moss asked President Harry S. Truman to release an engineering study on a proposal to link the city of Sacramento to the sea. Truman released the study, which had been withheld by opponents of the scheme. Congress eventually approved the plan, and in 1963 a 26-mile (42-km) shipping channel connected the city to the Sacramento River, which in turn ran to the Pacific Ocean.

Moss learned from the experience the vital importance of access to government documents. "[We] had a hell of a time getting any information," he said later, recalling Congress's battles to view pertinent papers and reports. Over the next twenty-six years as a member of Congress from California,

Father of the FOIA

Moss was the champion of the freedom of information cause on Capitol Hill.

Because of his tenacity in leading the fight for open government against leaders in both parties, Moss never made it to the higher rungs of power. In his early days as a member of Congress, Moss persuaded fellow Democrats to form a special subcommittee to investigate government secrecy and to appoint him as chairman. He later served as assistant Democratic floor leader. But that was as far as he got. After more than a quarter century of service in Congress, he never won appointment to chair any full committee.

Moss made enemies in high places. Cabinet members, agency heads, and high-ranking military officers testified against Moss's efforts to open their files. President Lyndon Johnson pressured him to drop his freedom of information campaign. By the time Moss died in 1997, the FBI had compiled a file two inches thick on the former congressman. Among the clippings in the file was a news article about Moss's criticism of a "silly cover-up" by the Air Force. The article, published in May 1958, quoted Moss as demanding a "full explanation" of the Air Force's attempts to keep secret the fact that researchers had placed a mouse aboard a failed research rocket launched the previous April.

Nevertheless, Moss exerted influence as chair of the Government Information Subcommittee. In addition to his work on the Freedom of Information Act, he helped push through an impressive list of consumer protection laws, including the Consumer Product Safety Commission, the Toy Safety Act, the Poison Package Control Act, and the first automobile lemon law. He also made major improvements to the Federal Trade Commission Act, which tightened securities regulations, and was instrumental in winning passage of the

Representative John Moss (*right*) confers with a group of newspaper editors and publishers before a Washington hearing on government's restrictions on information on March 19, 1963. From left: Walter B. Potter, publisher of the *Star-Exponent* in Culpeper, Virginia; Charles S. Rowe, editor of the *Free-Lance Star* in Fredericksburg, Virginia; and Gene Robb, publisher of the *Times-Union* and *Knickerbocker News* in Albany, New York. The newsmen demanded greater access to public records.

Federal Privacy Act. Consumer advocate Ralph Nader once called Moss "one of the greatest members of Congress of [the twentieth] century."

"I didn't back away from many challenges," Moss told a former staff member shortly before he died. "Sometimes you cannot compromise, you have to fight."

Other journalists criticized the government's policy of keeping even nonmilitary information from the press and the public. They noted that the press's job was to inform the public, so any attempts to keep information from the media worked against the public's right to know. "Whatever right the press has to information is a public right," said Richard W. Slocum, president of the American Newspaper Publishers Association. "We are the acting trustees of a public right."

A steady stream of agency heads testified against any attempt to open government records. Representatives from the Civil Service Commission declared that the agency had an inherent right to keep documents secret. At least seventeen other agencies based their authority to keep secrets on President Eisenhower's earlier claim of executive privilege for the Defense Department. Eisenhower had claimed the right to withhold "confidential matters within the Executive Department" during Senate hearings on the Army chaired by Senator Joseph McCarthy. Senators accepted the president's position and did not require former Army counsel John Adams to testify. Other agencies contended that the president had "stated a general principle of Government," which applied to all departments within the executive branch, not just those concerned with defense.

Moss's subcommittee revealed the creation of thirty new categories of classifications designed to keep government documents secret. The terms covered a myriad of circumstances not related to the nation's security. They included such labels as "need to know," "medical/private," "restricted to headquarters," and "restricted to use of principal staff." The American Battle Monuments Commission was the only agency among sixty executive departments that claimed it did not keep information from the public or the press.

The hearings continued through the winter, but Congress took no action on the issue. Moss stood firm in his belief that claims of national defense did not justify sealing most government documents. "The present trend toward Government secrecy could end in a dictatorship," Moss warned his colleagues in 1956. "The more information there is made available, the greater will be the nation's security."

"RED SCARE"

A large number of Americans, including many government officials, disagreed with Moss's assessment. They believed that communists threatened the nation and that opening government files would aid the enemy's efforts to undermine the United States. In the mid–1940s and early 1950s several international events occurred that fanned Americans' fear of a communist takeover.

During World War II the communist-controlled Soviet Union allied with the United States against Nazi Germany. However, the Soviet Union invaded a number of surrounding countries during and after the war and became the chief rival of the United States. The tension between the two nations escalated into the cold war and sparked threats of nuclear bomb attacks in the 1950s and 1960s. Communists won control of China in 1949 and later backed North Korea in its conflict with U.S.-sponsored South Korea. Young intellectuals and idealists in America and elsewhere in the 1920s and 1930s were attracted to the tenets of communism, which called for the sharing of labor and property among all members of the community. Many became disillusioned and quit the party, however, after despots in Russia, China, and other nations took over the Communist Party for their own purposes.

The 1951 trial and execution of American communists Ethel

and Julius Rosenberg as Soviet spies and the trial and perjury conviction of Alger Hiss, another American accused of espionage for the Soviets, intensified anticommunist sentiment in the United States. The red star on the Soviet flag became the symbol of communism worldwide.

The "Red Scare," as the anticommunist frenzy came to be known, swept across America, first in the late 1910s when communists gained control in Russia and later in the 1940s and 1950s. The Soviets exploded their first atomic bomb in 1949; four years later the Soviet Union successfully detonated a test hydrogen bomb. In response, the U.S. government ran an extensive information campaign on how Americans could prepare themselves for an atomic war and what steps they should take to survive such a catastrophe. Though meant to ease citizens' fears, these programs served to heighten Americans' awareness of the possibility of nuclear attack. During civil defense drills, warning signals blared from the nation's radios and schoolchildren were directed to hide under their desks. Many Americans became convinced that communists would bomb the United States in their quest for worldwide domination. They built bomb shelters (later determined to be useless) to protect their families in the event of a nuclear attack and lived in fear of a communist takeover.

Public hearings conducted in the Senate during the early 1950s by Senator Joseph McCarthy, a Republican from Wisconsin, further inflamed Americans' fears. McCarthy claimed that Soviet spies had overrun federal agencies. He conducted a witch hunt to root out communists and their sympathizers in the U.S. Army. Hurling unsubstantiated charges and abusive insults during the televised hearings, he bullied witnesses and destroyed reputations. The House Committee on Un-American Activities (HUAC) employed similar tactics in

Sixth-grade teacher Vincent M. Bohan (*left*) and his students at Public School 152 in New York City crouch beside their desks on Nov. 21, 1951, during an air-raid drill.

its investigation of the motion picture industry. As a result of HUAC's hearings, hundreds of people with no connection to the Soviet Union or the Communist Party lost their jobs and found themselves on a blacklist of enemies of the United States whom no one would hire.

The paranoia of the Red Scare that gripped Congress and the nation doomed Moss's campaign for open government—at least for a time. The Senate censured McCarthy for his bullying behavior in 1954, but it did not abandon its investigation of communists in America. During hearings held by the Senate's internal security subcommittee in late June 1955, CBS correspondent Winston Burdett revealed he had been a communist spy when he worked at the *Brooklyn Eagle* in the late 1930s. He named twelve former members of the *Eagle*'s staff who had belonged to the Communist Party. Burdett's sensational revelations and the subcommittee's subsequent questioning of news personnel tainted the press. As a result, Congress and the American public resisted efforts to open government secrets to reporters. Although investigations of communist subversives persisted into the early 1960s, Congress finally ended the aggressive, front-page grilling of suspects in the late 1950s after intense criticism from many U.S. leaders, including former president Harry S. Truman.

Information in secret government files released years later showed that communists did in fact infiltrate the U.S. government after World War II. The American public, Congress, and even President Truman never had access to that information at the time. Instead, anticommunists relied on the fantastic and unproven charges of politicians like Joseph McCarthy. That caused a backlash and undercut the credibility of those who warned against foreign espionage.

HOUSEKEEPING AMENDMENT

The censure of McCarthy, court rulings favorable to the press, and disgust over government tactics tipped the scales back toward public support of freedom of information. During hearings on the issue in 1957, Moss's subcommittee heard from lawyers, business owners, scientists, historians, labor leaders, and many others who supported the open government effort. They told of fruitless battles with federal agencies to inspect historical documents, business records, scientific findings, and a number of reports necessary to conduct their work. When Moss asked the federal agencies involved to justify withholding the materials, many cited the 1789 Housekeeping Act. Government officials had "twisted and tortured" the Housekeeping Act, Moss said, to use its provisions to withhold information from Congress and the public.

Moss found a strong ally in Senator Thomas C. Hennings, a

Missouri Democrat, who led the fight in the Senate for open government. Hennings chaired the Subcommittee on Constitutional Rights, which conducted hearings on whether the government's secrecy policies infringed on Americans' constitutional rights. The subcommittee reported many cases of what Hennings termed "clearly unwarranted withholdings of information from both the public and Congress by various government departments and agencies."

Both Hennings in the Senate and Moss in the House pushed for legislation that would allow Americans better access to government records. In 1957 they introduced bills to amend the Administrative Procedure Act. The bills, based on a study prepared by Jacob Scher, chief counsel to the Moss subcommittee, proposed major changes in the way federal bureaucracies handled information. The legislation guaranteed public access to government documents except in cases where national security would be endangered. The efforts of the two lawmakers, however, met with little success.

Moss and Hennings had better luck with a bill to amend the 1789 Housekeeping Act. The proposal merely added one sentence to the original law: "This section does not authorize withholding information from the public or limiting the availability of records to the public." Dubbed the "freedom of information" bill, the measure was designed to stop officials from using the old law to conceal information.

As mild as it was, the proposed legislation pitted the legislative branch (Congress) against the executive branch. All ten members of President Eisenhower's Cabinet took strong stands against the FOI amendment. They claimed that their departments had to keep documents secret to protect the nation. And they opposed the bill on the grounds that it would take away power from the executive branch.

On February 7, 1958, Wiggins and Cross both testified in support of the bill. The newsmen charged that government officials conducted public business behind a "paper curtain." On February 18, more than two years after Moss introduced the issue of government secrecy, his subcommittee voted unanimously to approve the amendment to the 1789 law. On April 16 the full House approved the Moss bill by voice vote.

Without much debate, the Senate passed the Hennings bill, and on August 12 a reluctant President Eisenhower signed the measure into law. Eisenhower made it clear, however, that heads of federal departments would still have the power to keep "appropriate information or papers" secret. "This power in the executive branch is inherent under the Constitution," Eisenhower noted in a statement after the signing.

Critics questioned whether the law would have much effect on government secrets. At least eighty laws authorizing government secrecy remained on the books. U.S. Attorney General William P. Rogers stated that the executive branch had a constitutional right to withhold any information it desired, regardless of any law Congress passed.

Moss himself acknowledged that the bill was "merely a first, timid step toward eradicating unnecessary Government secrecy." However, Moss saw in Congress's support of the bill a hopeful sign that other measures would win passage. "It demonstrates that Congress is aware of the growing threat of improper secrecy in Federal departments and agencies which involve virtually every facet of American life," he wrote in a *New York Times* article. The new law, Moss noted, also served "notice to Federal officials that unless they have clear statutory authority for withholding information the right to know shall prevail."

For Moss, the fight for open government had just begun.

Protesters against the Vietnam War hold signs attacking President Lyndon B. Johnson and Vice President Hubert H. Humphrey at a rally in New York City in October 1968. Citizens' opposition to the war—spurred by press reports and leaked documents critical of America's role in the conflict—pressured the U.S. government to withdraw from Vietnam.

CHAPTER THREE

Passage of the FOIA

As many commentators had predicted, the passage of the amendment to the Housekeeping Act did little to pry open government documents. Part of the problem lay with the government's classification system, which divided materials that were kept from public view into three main categories: confidential, secret, and top secret. Because each department or agency assigned classifications for its own records, the system was a jumble of different standards. By 1958 officials estimated the U.S. government held 2.6 billion sheets of secret documents. That equaled one sheet for every person living on the planet at that time.

The Defense Department held the most classified material, but each agency—for its own reasons—contributed a mountain of secret documents to the pile. Some of the hidden information had little to do with national security. Certain documents had already been made public by other sources. Often government officials themselves released classified information they believed would benefit themselves or their department. The press published reports based on such leaks. The system seldom punished insiders for leaks and had no way of penalizing those outside the government who made classified information public.

The increasingly unmanageable system had long been of concern for both Congress and the agencies of the federal government. In 1955 Congress passed a law ordering an investigation of the secrecy issue—the first ever authorized by federal law. The Commission on Protecting and Reducing Government Secrecy, headed by Loyd Wright, former president of the American Bar Association, studied the matter for the next eighteen months.

CALL FOR DECLASSIFICATION

While the congressional commission conducted its study, insiders in the Defense Department called for the declassification of many documents held there. Alarmed by leaks of sensitive information, officials believed the massive amount of classified materials made it harder to protect information vital to the nation's security. In 1956 Charles Wilson, the secretary of defense, formed a committee to find ways to stop leaks of classified information. Assistant Secretary of Defense Charles Coolidge chaired the committee, which was made up of retired military officers. The committee's report, issued on November 8, 1956, found the department's classification system to be "theoretically sound." But it noted that the tendency to overclassify materials (and keep them secret) had reached "serious proportions." Because many items had been unnecessarily marked *top secret* and withheld from the public, people had begun to lose confidence in the classification system, according to the report.

The danger of classifying too much material, the report stated, was that it undermined the entire system. "The press regards the stamp of classification with feelings which vary from indifference to active contempt," the report declared. Even Defense Department workers held "a casual attitude toward classified information." The overload of materials also strained the ability of the department to protect information that really should be kept secret.

The report described the dilemma of an open society:

> Being a democracy, the government cannot cloak its operations in secrecy. Adequate information as to its activities must be given to its citizens or the foundations of its democracy will be eaten away. . . . On the other hand, our democracy can be destroyed in another way, namely, by giving a potential enemy such information as will enable him to conquer us by war. A balance must be struck between these conflicting necessities.

The report listed a whole range of materials that had been classified in error: collections of materials already published, information already released by officials or accessible from other sources, nonmilitary personnel matters and advisers' comments, and information withheld because of a temporary foreign policy situation.

The best way to protect the nation's military secrets, the committee concluded, was to eliminate unnecessary materials from the classification system, including information "which cannot be held secret." The committee warned that the classification system should not to be used to hide "information not affecting the national security." The whole department, "from the Secretary of Defense down," should be committed to reducing the number of classified documents.

The committee also advised the Defense Department to appoint a special officer to declassify materials, to limit the people authorized to classify documents, and to develop more precise guidelines to determine when information should be kept secret. It also recommended dealing sternly with those who leaked classified materials.

In July 1957 Defense Secretary Wilson ordered a revamping of the department's classification system. Following the committee's recommendations, he told the armed forces to stop hiding information already publicly known. Wilson also limited the number of people within the department who could classify materials as top secret or secret. His directive, however, did not impose any penalties on those who classified materials that did not require secrecy. And it applied only to the Defense Department.

In June of that year the Commission on Protecting and Reducing Government Secrecy produced its eight-hundred-page report. In its initial statement, the report denounced the nation's security system as "a vast, intricate, confusing and costly complex of temporary, inadequate, uncoordinated programs and measures." As the Coolidge Committee had done, Congress's commission concluded that overclassification was a threat to the nation's security. The commission's major concern, however, was not about barriers to the public's right to know but about a system that could not protect state secrets and that hindered the "free exchange of ideas and information" essential to the nation's scientific and technological progress.

The commission's report recommended that the lowest rung of classification, the *confidential* category, be eliminated.

That would have left the *secret* and *top secret* rankings, which, the commission reasoned, adequately covered national security information. Only agency heads should be authorized to classify materials, the commission declared. The panel also advised creating a Central Security Office to review the system, supervise the declassification and handling of materials that posed no threat, and recommend changes when necessary. The commissioners noted that the president had the power to keep hidden the documents in the agencies under his control.

The report ended with proposals for two laws. One would make it a crime for anyone to disclose classified materials. This ban included people outside the government—including the press—as well as federal employees. The second proposal would authorize the courts to consider evidence collected by government wiretaps when trying those suspected of leaking information to the nation's enemies.

A storm of protest greeted the report. Members of the press attacked the first proposal on the grounds that it interfered with the press's right to publish, a violation of the First Amendment. The commission also found itself under attack from executive branch agencies. As noted in a report on secrecy issued more than four decades later, agencies held firmly to their secrets. They would not willingly allow an independent Central Security Office to change their policies:

> Secrets had become assets; organizations hoarded them, revealed them sparingly and in return for some consideration, and wanted no part of some Central Office busying itself with their internal affairs.

Several of the commission's proposals made their way to Congress, but lawmakers never seriously considered them. Ironically, the objections of the press helped to bury the proposal to declassify the *confidential* category of materials, which would have opened access to more information. The commission's other extensive recommendations were ignored as well.

Shortly after its formation, the Moss subcommittee began its own two-year effort to study the federal government's policies on classifying information. Like the two reports released in 1956 and 1957, the subcommittee's study found many abuses of the top secret and secret classifications. Issued on June 16, 1958, the Moss report recommended that independent arbiters review all complaints about classified materials; that classifications be reconsidered after a certain date and the materials declassified if possible; that the Defense Department be required to begin declassifying materials in its files; and that officials who classified too much material as top secret be punished.

THE BATTLE CONTINUES

Over the next several years Moss, Hennings, and others submitted a number of bills to establish a more open policy toward federal documents. None received much consideration, and neither house took action on the bills.

The push for open documents got a boost from a prestigious group of scientists in 1959. At the request of Senator Hennings, sixteen American scientists, all of whom had won Nobel Prizes, wrote letters stating that the government's policy on secrecy was hindering scientific development. The government's restrictions on information, they said, made it more difficult to cooperate with other scientists, damaged

Shh! It's a Secret!

During John Moss's long campaign to make government records public, his subcommittee on government information unearthed many examples of harmless information that federal agencies withheld. Under the Administrative Procedure Act, agency heads could deny access to materials if they determined the person making the request did not "need to know" the information. In recent times government officials continue to hide information for reasons that strain the credulity of even the most supportive observer. Among some of the materials agencies have refused to release:

- a textbook containing a description of George Washington's methods of collecting intelligence;
- a Confederate Army general's memoirs;
- a report on shark attacks and the use of shark repellents;
- telephone directories for the Pentagon;
- cost estimates prepared for nonsecret projects by unsuccessful bidders;
- a recipe for invisible ink developed in 1917;
- medical records for Ryma, a giraffe in the National Zoo.

morale, and discouraged leaders in research from coming to the United States.

"It just does not make sense to classify fundamental scientific information," wrote Walter H. Brattain, a physicist. In one case the results of a research project became obsolete before the government released the work for publication. "I feel very strongly that most restrictions done in the name of national security turn out to be foolish. . . . Don't kill the baby to protect it from the kidnappers." Only one scientist—

Dr. William P. Murphy, a Nobel Prize–winning physician—supported the government's secrecy system. He said that restrictions on information had a "rather minimal" effect on scientific advances.

Senator Hennings died of abdominal cancer in September 1960. Edward Long, also a Democrat, was appointed to fill Hennings's seat and took up the cause of freedom of information in the Senate.

In September Jacob Scher, chief counsel to the Moss subcommittee, presented a draft of yet another bill designed to open access to public records. The new bill amended the Administrative Procedure Act and contained five major provisions. First, it eliminated the vague wording of the Administrative Procedure Act of 1946 and required specific reasons (not just "good cause") to categorize documents as secret. Second, the legislation for the first time guaranteed the right of Americans to view public records. Third, the act gave *anyone* the right to request information; it did not limit access to people who had a proven interest in the material. Fourth, citizens would have the right to pursue their request for information in court if agencies denied access. And fifth, federal officials would have to give good reasons—specified in the law—to keep a document under wraps. The legislation allowed officials not to disclose documents that had to be kept secret to protect the national defense, records already withheld under other laws, and private information (such as medical or other records) not connected to the government.

Like the previous bills, this one did not get far.

NEW ADMINISTRATION: SUNSHINE AND SECRETS

Moss withstood incredible forces in his battle for freedom of information. Members of Congress threatened to cut off funding for his subcommittee. President Eisenhower and his Republican allies opposed moves to force the executive branch to open its records. Every member of the president's Cabinet testified against Moss's bill, and officials from 105 federal agencies went on record opposing the legislation. In Moss's view, such objections by the executive branch proved that the administration and its agencies would never willingly open its files and that it was up to Congress to force the federal government to allow public access to documents.

Democrats as well as Republicans stood in the way of Moss's antisecrecy efforts. As the powerful Senate majority leader, Lyndon B. Johnson offered no help in the fight against secrecy. Nevertheless, Johnson pledged the "fullest possible freedom of public information" after becoming vice president in the 1960 election. Moss expressed hope that the freedom of information campaign would benefit from having a Democrat in the White House.

One promising move took place in 1961 when President Kennedy set up a system to automatically declassify records in government files. Moss's subcommittee had lobbied for the declassification system since 1958. Under the system, federal agencies were required to review documents on a regular basis and declassify those they decided no longer needed to be kept secret. Moss called it "a major improvement in the information protection system." A year later, however, Moss reported that, even with the system in place, government agencies continued to withhold information that had been cleared by other agencies. As an example, he cited the State Department's refusal to release a study on efforts to put an American on the moon, despite recommendations by the army to declassify an edited version of the study.

In 1962, after several federal agencies rebuffed Moss's

attempt to view their records, the congressman persuaded Kennedy to promise that only the president would invoke executive privilege to keep documents hidden. Moss later secured a similar pledge from President Johnson. The press, however, saw few advances in the campaign for an open government under the Kennedy administration. The Freedom of Information Committee, organized by Sigma Delta Chi, a national organization of journalists, reported in the fall of 1962 that there had been "no major change in the bureaucratic censorship" since Kennedy had taken office. Kennedy had "expressed doubt," in a letter written to the group, that a law could deal with the problem of open government, the group's chairman said. State and local governments had made much more progress in opening meetings and documents to the public, the journalist noted.

In mid–October 1962 President Kennedy learned that the Soviet Union was building nuclear missile sites on Cuba, only 90 miles (145 km) from the U.S. shore. Kennedy ordered U.S. ships to form a blockade around the island nation to prevent the Soviets from delivering missiles to Cuba. The incident took the nations—and the world—to the brink of a nuclear war. Fortunately, the Soviets withdrew their missiles and an armed conflict was avoided. Secret papers documenting the incident, declassified decades later, revealed U.S. covert operations to overthrow Cuban president Fidel Castro, Soviet resentment over U.S. missiles in Turkey, and dangerous missteps and misunderstandings on both sides that almost led to all-out warfare. At the time, however, the Kennedy administration successfully portrayed the president's handling of the crisis as "brilliantly controlled" and "matchlessly calibrated," in the words of Kennedy's biographer, Arthur Schlesinger Jr. The administration buried government records that showed otherwise, asserting that secrecy was necessary to protect national security. As a result of this effective public relations campaign, Kennedy's approval ratings among Americans soared to 74 percent. The administration's policy of keeping documents secret, however, infuriated the press and renewed calls for a law to allow public access to government records.

In March 1963 Moss's subcommittee again opened hearings on government secrecy. The committee sought to set guidelines on how to separate truly sensitive material from documents that could be safely—and legitimately—viewed by the public. The first sessions focused on charges that the Kennedy Administration was "managing" the news. Members of the media testified that by distorting the truth, the administration not only damaged its credibility but also

Customers in a California store listen to President John F. Kennedy's televised address to Americans informing them about the Cuban missile crisis on October 22, 1962.

undermined the people's trust in their government. "A government can successfully lie no more than once to its people," testified Gene Robb, vice president of the American Newspaper Publishers Association. "Thereafter everything it says and does becomes suspect. All the more so when a high-ranking government officer makes speeches to justify these lies."

Two top-ranking officials from the Kennedy administration, who testified later that month, defended the government's need to keep secrets during dangerous situations to protect the nation. Arthur Sylvester, assistant secretary of defense for public affairs, told the committee that "in times of crisis information which ordinarily would be made available to our citizens must temporarily be withheld in order to deny it to our enemies." Critics had assailed Sylvester earlier for keeping information from the press during the Cuban missile crisis. He later said the government was justified in "lying" if it protected the nation from nuclear war. A State Department official expressed similar views during his testimony. "There are moments when the interests of the Government serving the people and a press informing the people do not coincide," said Robert J. Manning, the official in charge of public affairs for the State Department.

DEBATE AND DELAYS

In May Moss's subcommittee was forced to hold its first closed hearing when it quizzed military leaders on secrecy issues. The panel discussed the handling of news about South Vietnam and the rising tension there. The move brought apologies from Moss, who had never before held a secret session of the subcommittee in the eight years it had operated.

After the session, Moss announced that Americans were

receiving as much news "as is possible about the battle against Communist guerrillas in South Vietnam." That assurance evaporated, however, when Moss's subcommittee discovered that the State Department had ordered U.S. officials in Vietnam not to share information on military operations or allow American reporters to go on maneuvers that might lead to unfavorable news reports. Kennedy rescinded the policy in the spring of 1963.

According to the committee's report on the matter, issued in September 1963, the policy kept the American people from understanding the situation in Vietnam. In 1963 U.S. forces in South Vietnam numbered more than 16,000, and the Viet Cong were gaining support from villagers opposed to the South Vietnam regime of president Ngo Dinh Diem. In January 1963 the U.S.–backed South Vietnamese army lost its first major battle against the Viet Cong, who later took control of the Mekong Delta. "Instead of hiding the facts from the American public, the State Department should have done everything possible to expose the true situation to full view," the subcommittee's report read. The State Department's "restrictive press policy in Vietnam," the report continued, was drafted "by an official with an admitted distrust for the people's right to know" and "unquestionably contributed to the lack of information about conditions in Vietnam which created an international crisis."

Both the House and the Senate considered freedom of information bills in 1963. The House bill, approved by Moss's subcommittee, went to the House Judiciary Committee for review in mid–1963 before going to the Rules Committee and then to the full House for debate. Under pressure from opponents of the bill, the Judiciary Committee held the bill for more than a year with no action.

In the Senate, Edward Long made better progress in his fight to pass a freedom of information bill. He and Senate Minority Leader Everett Dirksen introduced a bill that would have replaced the APA entirely. A second bill, introduced by Long and cosponsored by twenty-one senators including Dirksen, amended Section Three of the APA, which allowed the public to view agencies' records but contained many loopholes that interfered with the public's access to such materials. Senators who supported open access wanted to make sure that Congress passed a bill, one way or the other, that would ease restrictions on government records.

The Senate Judiciary Committee's Subcommittee on Administrative Practice and Procedure, headed by Long, opened hearings on the bills in October 1963. Long said legislation was needed because "too much of the public's business is being conducted in virtual secrecy." The senator declared, in opening the hearings, "Free people are, of necessity, informed; uninformed people can never be free."

Agency heads strongly objected to the bills, which allowed exemptions only for information related to national security. The officials argued that confidential intraoffice communications (for example, personnel matters) should not be released to the public. They also expressed concern over disclosing sensitive information that could affect the nation's relations with foreign countries. The committee rejected the more ambitious bill and focused on the amendment to the APA. Long, a realist, held little hope that even that bill would pass in its present form. "We should not kid ourselves about the legislation's prospects," he told the press. "There is intense opposition to the bill from virtually every government agency in Washington."

That fall the Freedom of Information Committee, in its

1963 report on open government, declared that access to federal documents had reached "the lowest ebb in history." The Defense Department, according to the report, was the worst offender, but other agencies and departments as well as Congress came in for their share of criticism for "spreading . . . the blanket of secrecy over the records of government, and particularly over those records pertaining to spending of taxpayer funds."

The report urged Congress to pass a law that would force government departments and agencies to open their records—except those related to national security—to the public. Representative Moss would carry out that directive, at least partially, but it would take him almost three more years to accomplish the feat. Before that happened, a tragedy—and the swearing in of a new president—would intervene.

MOSS UNDER FIRE

On November 22, 1963, Lee Harvey Oswald shot and killed President Kennedy as his motorcade passed through the streets of Dallas, Texas. Two hours later Vice President Lyndon B. Johnson, who had been riding in the same motorcade, took the oath of office on board Air Force One. The new president pledged to continue Kennedy's commitment to civil rights, the space program, the Vietnam War, and other projects. His administration, like Kennedy's, resisted efforts to open government documents to the press and the public, particularly those managed by the Defense Department.

No president wanted to give up control over the documents in the many departments and agencies of the executive branch. No president wanted embarrassing information about the administration to be displayed to the public. Democrat Lyndon B. Johnson was no different from presidents before him when it came to wanting to keep a lid on certain information under his control. He sought to hide information about U.S. involvement in Vietnam, in particular, that would have bolstered criticism of his administration over the handling of the controversial war in Southeast Asia. During John Moss's campaign to pass a comprehensive Freedom of Information Act, President Johnson and officials in his administration did what they could to stop the legislation.

"The negotiations were very rough," Moss said later when discussing the FOIA. "I recall that the assistant attorney general would walk out and say, 'All right, there'll be no bill, then.'" Moss said the Justice Department implied that the president would veto the bill if it passed without major revisions.

At one point during the hearings, House Speaker John McCormack signaled to Moss to confer with him. The Democratic leader made it clear that President Johnson wanted Moss to "defer" the bill. The congressman made it known that he would not defer the bill or defer to the president. Lesser opponents did not survive such a confrontation with Johnson, a master politician who knew how to wield power to get his way and who held a grudge with an iron grip. But Moss had an even greater power on his side—the power of public opinion, which Johnson did not want to ruffle. The president needed the wholehearted support of Americans in his effort to pass the many programs in his Great Society campaign. Asked years later about the incident, Moss confided that he knew his actions would not sit well with Johnson, but he did not alter his course. "I did what I had to do," he said.

With his bill languishing in the Judiciary Committee, Moss continued to wage the campaign in the press. In May 1964 he related unsuccessful efforts to pry details about several government projects that Congress was supposed to oversee.

The federal agencies in charge of the projects refused to release the terms of the contracts, how contractors were chosen, or any other details about the deals. Without such information, Congress could not determine whether an award was part of a political deal or whether the price was inflated. Moss targeted the Defense Department as the biggest offender in making secret deals. "In defense," he said, "it is so easy to cloak everything on security grounds. . . . It is also so difficult to know what legitimate information might be available. Defense has tried to control all sources of information." Moss urged news reporters and others to file complaints about withheld information as a way to highlight the problem.

In the Senate, Long's subcommittee held hearings on a new version of the freedom of information bill in July 1964. The amended bill, which addressed only Section Three of the APA, included a long list of exemptions to ease the concerns of federal officials. The changes aimed to win support from agencies that had resisted the bill, but it also weakened the act and provided loopholes for officials looking for a way to avoid disclosures.

The Senate Judiciary Committee approved the revised bill on July 21, 1964, and recommended that the full Senate pass the measure. A week later the Senate, without debate, passed its version of the bill by voice vote. The bill died when the House took no action on it. That did not mean, however, that Moss had abandoned the fight.

BIPARTISAN COALITION PUSHES BILL

When the next Congress took office in 1965, Moss and Long joined forces and, with the support of a bipartisan coalition of senators and House members, vowed to push through a freedom of information bill. Moss had originally hoped to pass a bill that allowed few exceptions to the open access policy. But the California lawmaker recognized the political realities facing him. To win Senate support of the bill and present a united front, he agreed to nine categories of records that the government could keep secret:

- Classified information on national defense or foreign policy.
- Internal rules on the personnel and the practices of an agency.
- Materials to be kept secret under other laws.
- Trade secrets and confidential financial data on individual Americans and corporations.
- Privileged information from court proceedings.
- Medical and personnel files that would amount to an invasion of a person's privacy.
- Files compiled by law enforcement agents on an ongoing investigation.
- Confidential data on financial institutions.
- Materials relating to the geology and geography of oil wells.

On February 17, 1965, Moss and Long introduced identical bills in the House and the Senate. Twenty-five members of both parties signed on as cosponsors. Both bills incorporated the basics of the previous legislation guaranteeing access to government records and giving citizens the right to go to court if access were denied.

Members of the press and the media continued to support the bill. The Johnson administration and the departments and agencies under the executive branch renewed their opposition to it. Twenty-seven agencies and departments sent officials to speak against the bill during the subcommittee's hearings.

Moss's subcommittee ended its hearings on the bill in April. In the months that followed, members revised the bill eight times to try to win the support of the Johnson administration. The campaign received help from a surprising source. Donald Rumsfeld, then a young Republican from Illinois in his first term in the House, lobbied for the bill as a member of Moss's subcommittee. Rumsfeld, who signed on as a cosponsor of the FOIA, and other Republicans, who had opposed the bill under a Republican president, saw a political benefit in opening the records of the Democratic administration of Lyndon B. Johnson.

Even with the nine exemptions in place, President Johnson and officials in his administration tried to scuttle the bill. The Justice Department, which led the administration's opposition to the bill, pushed for a clause that guaranteed the president's right, under executive privilege, to withhold any documents the administration decided should not be made public. The Justice officials argued that without the clause, the bill would upset the balance of power—and violate the Constitution—by not giving the president control over executive branch affairs.

This time, however, Moss did not bow to the pressure. He refused to go along with the Justice Department's demands, which would have gutted the bill and allowed the administration to exclude any materials it did not want released. "I will not agree to any language that grants statutory recognition to executive privilege," he told reporters in August.

Long's subcommittee held its hearings on the bill in May. On October 1, 1965, the Senate Judiciary Committee gave the measure its support and urged the act's passage. "Although the theory of an informed electorate is vital to the proper operation of a democracy, there is now nowhere in our present law a statute which affirmatively provides for that information," the committee noted in a statement to the Senate. On October 13 senators passed the Freedom of Information Act without debate on a voice vote. By taking a voice vote, in which members said "yea" or "nay," the senators avoided the lengthy process of registering their votes one by one. In a voice vote, there is no record of how an individual member of Congress has voted.

With Congress about to recess, Moss told reporters that his committee would consider the Senate version of the bill at the beginning of the new year. In March 1966 Moss's subcommittee unanimously approved a measure that duplicated the one passed by the Senate. Committee member Rumsfeld explained why Republicans as well as Democrats supported the legislation: "The unanimous action after years of delay results from the growing size and complexity of the federal government, from its increased role in our lives and from the increasing awareness by Americans of the threat involved in government secrecy on vital records affecting their fate."

The full House Committee on Government Operations took similar action, approving the bill by unanimous vote on April 27. The bill came before the House in June for a final vote on the matter. By this time, thirty-seven states had passed their own freedom of information laws similar to the federal statute. Members of the House recognized that public sentiment supported the measure. In an unusual move the House agreed to deal directly with the bill, instead of following procedure and requiring it to pass through the House Judiciary and Rules Committees. By doing so, representatives had to pass the bill by at least a two-thirds margin instead of a simple majority. By then, Moss and his colleagues had little doubt the bill would pass with the required number of votes.

Representatives devoted little more than an hour of discussion to the legislation. No one spoke against the bill. On June 20—twelve years after he began his campaign for open government—Moss quietly celebrated as the bill passed the House on a vote of 307 to 0. One hundred twenty-five representatives did not vote on the measure. However, of those not voting, 124 paired their votes. Sixty-two members who would have supported the measure had they voted paired off with sixty-two other members whose votes would have been against the bill. The *Congressional Record* lists these pairings as part of the official report, although the pairs are not counted in the total vote. Members of Congress use the technique when they cannot cast their vote in person but want to record how they would have voted (although positions are not listed, one or both members' views are usually well known). By pairing their votes, members can also show voters back home that their absence made no difference in the final outcome of the legislation.

Moss, explaining the unanimous vote, said that supporters of freedom of information had to "develop a public dialog" on the issue before the bill could pass. "You had to educate the American people and the Congress itself on the need for such legislation," Moss said. He also credited the support of Republicans, who had called for public access to government documents during the 1964 presidential campaign. Republicans used the issue as a way to discredit President Johnson, who they claimed had controlled the news and kept the public in the dark about the U.S. role in Vietnam. Discussion of the issue during the campaign helped build support for the legislation, according to Moss.

AN AMERICAN MILESTONE

The only step left was for the president to sign the bill. Public support for the concept of open government made it difficult for Johnson to publicly oppose the law. Rumsfeld, a leader in the Republican campaign for the FOIA, noted that the policies of the Johnson administration made people aware of the need for the law. "With the continuing tendency toward managed news and suppression of public information that the people are entitled to have, the issues have at last been brought home forcefully to the public," Rumsfeld said.

Newspapers in practically every major U.S. city ran editorials calling for Johnson to sign the bill. "Freedom of speech and freedom of press are guaranteed by the Constitution. But . . . those are pretty empty guarantees unless accompanied by freedom of information," wrote an editor at the *Los Angeles Times*, echoing the words of Harold Cross more than a decade earlier. The *Arizona Republic*, among many others, touted "the right of a free people to know how their elected representatives [and their designated agents] are conducting the public business."

Even faced with overwhelming support for the bill, Johnson made Moss and his supporters sweat it out a little longer. Finally, on July 4, 1966—the last day before the bill would expire—Johnson gritted his teeth and signed the Freedom of Information Act. The president's press secretary, Bill Moyers, later revealed that Johnson had to be "dragged kicking and screaming" to the signing. Like many in the high reaches of power, Johnson wanted to protect his realm and did not relish having every action, document, and debate open to public scrutiny. "He hated the very idea of the Freedom of Information Act," said Moyers in a retrospective documentary aired by PBS in 2002. "He hated the thought of journalists

Press secretary Bill Moyers (*left*) meets with President Lyndon B. Johnson in the Oval Office of the White House in November 1963, shortly after Johnson assumed the presidency.

rummaging in government closets; hated them challenging the official view of reality." According to Moyers, Johnson agreed to sign the bill only after several last-minute calls from newspaper editors, who urged his support.

The signing took place at the president's ranch in Texas without fanfare. In his statement for the press, Johnson asserted that he had signed the measure "with a deep sense of pride that the United States is an open society in which the people's right to know is cherished and guarded." But in his signing statement, in which the president declared his interpretation of the new law, Johnson emphasized the need for government to keep some secrets. He included military information, personnel records, and advisers' communications on the list of information to be "protected from disclosure." In explaining the law, Johnson wrote, "The welfare of the Nation or the rights of individuals may require that some documents not be made available. Moreover, this bill in no way impairs the President's power under our Constitution to provide for confidentiality when the national interest so requires." He instructed officials in his administration to make records available "to the full extent consistent with individual privacy and with the national interest." Officials would later use Johnson's language in the signing statement to avoid demands for disclosure of public documents.

Under the terms of the legislation, the act became effective one year after the signing. The delay gave agencies time to develop procedures to be followed when someone requested records under the FOIA.

Moss, savoring victory after twelve long years, considered the law an American milestone. "For the first time in the nation's history," he said, "the people's right to know the facts of government will be guaranteed." But Moss had no illusions that the government's agencies would rush to open their records once the bill went into effect. He told reporters that the bill's "most important" feature was a provision that allowed citizens to sue for the right to view public documents. "It is this device," he said, "which expands the rights of the citizens and which protects them against arbitrary and capricious denials."

CHAPTER FOUR

FOIA Revisions

By 1969 the federal government maintained around 70 billion sheets of paper. Americans, armed with the Freedom of Information Act, slowly began to mine those records. Businesses and consumer groups became the first major users to take advantage of the FOIA. Many requests for documents initially came from businesses wanting access to government data on their industry, on competitors, and on clients. In the first two years after the law went into effect in 1967, the Department of Health, Education, and Welfare received ninety-five formal requests for information. Most came from the tobacco industry, which asked to see government data on smoking and health. In 1966 Congress had passed a law requiring tobacco companies to place a warning on all cigarette packages that smoking was harmful to health. Other laws were in the works that would limit advertising on television and radio. The Surgeon General had also issued reports on the hazards of cigarette smoking. Presumably,

Consumer advocate Ralph Nader (*left*) supervises a group of protesters in Washington, D.C., in October 1969. Public Citizen, the watchdog organization Nader founded in 1971, and other advocacy groups use the FOIA to gain access to information to advance their causes in the press and in court.

the cigarette companies wanted a firsthand look at the data used by the government in the studies.

During that time, the courts reviewed forty cases involving FOIA requests. Only three dealt with issues that affected a broad range of people. The bulk of the cases concerned private business matters, such as a bank's efforts to use public records to track down a client who owed the bank money.

The FOIA soon became an important tool of consumer advocate groups that wanted to gain access to government data on product safety and other topics. The industry watchdog group Consumers Union, publisher of *Consumer Reports*, was among the first to go to court under the FOIA. As a result of the group's suit, the Veterans Administration had to turn over its studies on hearing aids. Consumer advocate Ralph Nader announced in 1969 that he planned to sue in several cases involving government secrets. "Information, particularly timely information, is the currency of power," Nader said.

Surprisingly, given the press's strident support of the FOIA, no member of the media sued for information under the act in the first two years after it became effective. Members of the press noted that it often took weeks (or longer) to gain access to government documents—too long to meet news media deadlines. Instead of waiting for FOIA access, they relied on their own investigations, used information from other sources, and followed up on leaks—methods that had been used by the press for years. That disappointed some observers, who had hoped the act would aid reporters in uncovering important information about the government. "The press hasn't used the tool [FOIA]," said Samuel J. Archibald of the University of Missouri's Freedom of Information Center in 1969. "It's going to rust if it isn't used."

Some claimed the law's nine exemptions, and not a lack of journalistic interest in it, made the FOIA an ineffective tool. An investigation of the law conducted by the *New York Times* in 1969 found that officials had concealed under various exemptions a broad range of information, from "the fat content of hot dogs," to violations by moving companies, to studies on water pollution caused by federal plants, to the automobile industry's pricing structure.

Some agency heads reasoned that if they turned over information about private companies stored in their files, businesses would stop providing the data needed for government projects and reports. Other officials were hesitant to release raw data, which they feared would be misinterpreted.

DOCUMENTS STILL SECRET

Although the FOIA broke ground in allowing average citizens to take their appeals to court, it required patience— and money—to follow all the procedures and then sue if the agencies turned down a FOIA request. Some departments were more helpful than others. The Department of Health, Education, and Welfare, for example, set up an office specifically to deal with FOIA requests. The office approved sixty-six requests and denied twenty-nine in the first two years after the law went into effect. Other departments, like the Department of the Interior, resisted attempts to disclose reports related to consumer products and safety.

Ten years after the passage of the FOIA, Congressman John E. Moss assessed the law's effectiveness. "Vast amounts of material were routinely withheld [before FOIA]," he noted. "If you compare it with today, we've made vast progress." But he added, "If you ask me if we've made enough [progress], the answer is no."

Despite the passage of the FOIA, many government documents remained hidden from public view. In 1971, five years after the law's passage, *Time* magazine reported that the FOIA's effect on the government's information policies had been "almost nil." Officials used a number of tactics to keep records secret. National security and foreign policy claims covered a wide range of topics that were off-limits to the public. A vast array of materials, military and nonmilitary, were classified as secret and put under lock and key, inaccessible even to members of Congress and government agents in different departments. Presidents used executive privilege to avoid disclosing information they wanted to conceal. Officials buried other documents under a mountain of red tape. These measures all served to circumvent the provisions for open government promised by the FOIA.

In the 1960s and early 1970s, government officials kept the details of the Vietnam War wrapped in secrecy under the cloak of national security. The policy of secrecy led people to distrust the government and triggered a wave of protest against the war and the administration. Also, secret government operations and pacts committed the United States to large payments to foreign countries and pledges of military aid in the event of war—all without the knowledge of the U.S. citizens footing the bill. The Pentagon Papers, which were leaked to the press by military analyst Daniel Ellsberg, revealed an intricate web of deceit that showed that government officials from the president on down had lied to the American people about the Vietnam War. Even Congress did not receive a full account of U.S. dealings in the war.

Other secret government operations came to light during investigations conducted by the Senate Foreign Relations Subcommittee headed by Senator Stuart Symington, a Democrat from Missouri, in the early 1970s. The subcommittee uncovered the secret bombing of Laos by U.S. aircraft and the expenditure of millions of U.S. dollars in military aid to Laos leaders begun in the mid–1960s. The committee also found secret pacts U.S. officials had made with Ethiopia beginning in 1960 that required the United States to pay $159 million for weapons for the African nation's 40,000-member army. Under terms of the agreements, the U.S. government also provided military advisers to train Ethiopia's troops. David Newsom, the assistant secretary of state, testified that the administration had kept the agreements secret to protect the "great sensitivity" of Ethiopia's emperor, Haile Selassie. Neither Congress nor the American public knew of the arrangements.

Officials locked up nonmilitary information as well, by classifying it "not for distribution." In some cases, other government agencies could not do their work properly because they had no access to essential documents. In 1971, for example, a division of the Interior Department blocked agents of the U.S. Water Pollution Control Administration from viewing papers on offshore oil drilling in the Gulf of Mexico during their investigation of a fire on one of the drilling platforms.

Official red tape often stymied the efforts of public service organizations to use government research to back their claims. It took seven years for environmentalists to win the release of a government report on industrial wastes discharged into the nation's waterways. Other pertinent research findings remained buried indefinitely. An editorial in *Time* magazine in 1971 noted that disclosing government dealings to the public was the only way to increase "confidence and tranquillity between those who govern and those who are governed." The writer acknowledged the need for military secrets, but also noted that secrecy often served "as an easy cover for operational failures, as a mask for individual or collective mistakes in policymaking, as a shield for actual wrongdoing and as a cloak to hide the undertaking of new and often costly commitments." Not only did such secrecy damage the public's trust in government, it also made different branches of the government distrustful of one another. "Total and complete disclosure, particularly in dangerous times, represents an impossible dream," the writer

Outgoing president Lyndon B. Johnson (*left*) and incoming president Richard M. Nixon (*right*) confer in the Oval Office of the White House on January 20, 1969.

concluded. "But excessive secrecy is a contagious disease that could be fatal to the practice of modern democracy itself."

OPENING THE "CURTAINS OF SECRECY"
By 1972 supporters of open government had begun lobbying for a tougher Freedom of Information Act. As a report prepared by the Senate Subcommittee on Administrative Practice and Procedure would later note, the FOIA had become a

"freedom from information" law. The act relied on the "sound judgment and faithful execution" of agency officials, who set policy for their departments and determined whether information fell under the law's exemptions or could be released. Because those officials' fulfillment of the act's goals had been "substantially less than 'faithful,'" the report declared that "the curtains of secrecy still remain tightly drawn around the business of our government."

Citizens' opposition to the Vietnam War and criticism of his administration helped persuade President Lyndon Johnson not to seek reelection in 1968. Newly elected President Richard M. Nixon pledged to operate an "open administration." Ironically, revelations of Nixon's secret "dirty tricks" campaign to win reelection in 1972 highlighted the need for a stronger FOIA. During the Watergate scandal that followed, Nixon refused to turn over tape recordings of conversations in the Oval Office. In a rare break with tradition, the U.S. Supreme Court ordered the president to relinquish the tapes. The conversations revealed the administration's involvement in—or at least advance knowledge of—a break-in at the Democratic Party's offices, bagmen, and secret payoffs. These disclosures eventually drove Nixon from office in 1974. In another landmark decision, the Court ruled that newspapers could publish the Pentagon Papers. The scandal and the Court rulings deepened support for a tougher FOIA.

Lower court rulings also helped persuade Congress that the FOIA needed to be amended. Six years after the FOIA went into effect, more than two hundred suits to release information had been filed in court. Most decisions reinforced Congress's intent in passing the law to provide citizens with the information they needed to make intelligent decisions about their government. In many of the cases,

Representative Patsy Mink meets with reporters on Capitol Hill in 1997. Mink and other members of Congress lost their bid to use the FOIA to force the Environmental Protection Agency to turn over records on nuclear testing after the Supreme Court ruled in the agency's favor in a 1973 decision.

judges ordered officials to allow wide latitude in granting access to records and to keep records closed only in narrow circumstances as allowed under the law. Courts were more reluctant, however, to release information that the president claimed should be kept secret "in the interest of the national defense or foreign policy." They also were more likely to rule against disclosing records involved in law enforcement.

The Supreme Court almost always sided with the government on FOIA cases involving national security. In its first decision on a FOIA case, the Supreme Court put a major hurdle in the path of access to government records. In 1971 Representative Patsy Mink, a Democrat from Hawaii, and thirty-two other members of Congress demanded that President Nixon turn over nine documents on a planned underground nuclear test. When the administration refused to release the records, the lawmakers took the case to court under the FOIA. Federal officials claimed that the documents, held by the Environmental Protection Agency (EPA), were exempt. The records, according to the government, did not have to be disclosed because they contained privileged advice and recommendations to the president and involved "sensitive" information "vital to the national defense and foreign policy." In 1973 the Supreme Court ruled in favor of the administration in the case, *EPA* v. *Mink*. In a 5-to-3 decision, the Court decided that the president had the authority to determine whether materials qualified for exemption under the FOIA. The court also ruled that the president could delegate that authority to the agencies and departments in his administration. The justices overruled a lower court that had authorized district judges to examine classified documents and rule if they should remain secret.

TOUGH NEW AMENDMENTS

With the growing number of complaints about government secrecy, it was obvious the FOIA had not lived up to its name. In a series of hearings conducted in 1972 to 1974 in the House by Congressman Moss's old subcommittee (now known as the Subcommittee on Foreign Operations and Government Information), witnesses described numerous ways government officials blocked FOIA requests:

- Charged high fees for copying documents (up to $1 a page) and added an hourly charge for agency employees who had to find the records.

- Denied access to indexes maintained by the agency that would help locate papers.
- Mixed classified and nonclassified information in one file and refused to sort the materials.
- Refused to release materials similar to those ruled accessible by the courts, forcing petitioners to sue for access again and again.
- Delayed responding to requests for information; the long delays made it impossible for the press to rely on the FOIA for their news articles.
- Failed to adopt regulations that supported the FOIA and failed to tell citizens of their rights under the FOIA. Many agencies operated under policies that discouraged open government.

In February 1973 Pennsylvania Democrat William S. Moorhead, who had taken over as chair of the House sub-committee, and Republican Frank Horton of New York, both introduced bills to strengthen the FOIA. These bills were later merged into one. The House Government Operations Committee released the results of a two-year study in May of that year detailing the abuses of the classification system that kept public documents unnecessarily secret. The federal government's overclassification of documents cost taxpayers more than $100 million a year to handle and store the records, protect them from leaks, and later, to declassify them and transport them to other locations, the study reported.

In the Senate, the Subcommittee on Administrative Prac-tice and Procedure, headed by Senator Edward M. Kennedy of Massachusetts, began work on amendments to the FOIA to clarify and strengthen the law. In a report prepared for Congress, the subcommittee noted that the FOIA had helped change agencies' policies on the disclosure of information. Nevertheless, the subcommittee noted, the federal government continued to withhold records. "The expectation of Congress that the doors of government would be opened to the public has not been fully realized," Kennedy wrote in an introduction to the report.

In February 1974 the Senate subcommittee approved a bill to amend the FOIA and submitted it to the Judiciary Committee for review. The House Committee on Government Operations reported favorably on a similar bill the same month. On March 14 the full House voted a lopsided 383 to 8 to pass the measure. The most important provision of the bill amended the FOIA to allow a federal judge to review classified records in cases where the government denied access. If the judge determined that information had been withheld inappropriately, the documents could be released. The House included the provision to override the Supreme Court's decision in *EPA* v. *Mink*. "This bill offers a sensible and workable compromise between a Democratic government and the Government's need for national security," said Representative Spark M. Matsunaga, a Democrat from Hawaii, during the debate on the bill. Both the Defense Department and the Justice Department lobbied against the legislation.

The Senate passed its version of the bill with another large majority, 64 to 17. Like the House measure, the Senate bill included a provision to allow federal judges to review classified material. Senator Kennedy, who sponsored the bill, hailed the vote. "We have seen too much secrecy in the past few years, and the American people are tired of it," Kennedy declared. Republican Senator Howard H. Baker Jr. of Tennessee later noted that much of the material marked *classified* failed to meet the standards for such secrecy. "I reviewed

Senator Edward M. Kennedy (*left*) shakes the hand of Representative John E. Moss at the congressman's retirement party in the Rayburn House Office Building in Washington, D.C., in 1978.

literally hundreds of Watergate-related documents that had been classified 'secret' or 'top secret.' It is my opinion that at least 95 percent of these documents should not have been classified in the first place," Baker said. Despite the over-whelming show of support for the legislation, President Nixon warned that he might veto the bill.

After passage, the two bills went to conference to iron out differences in the House and Senate versions. In order for legislation to become law, both the House and the Senate have to pass identical bills. If the bills passed by the two houses are different, members from the House and the Senate hold a conference to work on a compromise bill. The revised bill is then presented to the House and the Senate for final approval.

The FOIA compromise bill consisted of seventeen amendments to the original legislation. The final bill authorized judges to review classified material and required the government to pay court costs of those who successfully sued to gain access to information. It also gave departments ten days to rule on a request for information and an additional twenty days to respond to an appeal. They would have thirty days to reply to a lawsuit filed to gain access to information. Officials who did not comply faced punishment. The new provisions also opened more law enforcement records. Under the bill, officials could withhold records only if their disclosure interfered with an ongoing case or hindered a person's right to a fair trial, invaded personal privacy, named a confidential source, put the lives of law enforcement officers at risk, or revealed police techniques. The bill required every agency to publish an index of its materials and set up standard fees for copying and searches.

By the time the conference approved the compromise in late August, Richard Nixon had resigned the presidency to avoid impeachment because of the Watergate scandal and Vice President Gerald Ford had taken over. The disclosure of Nixon's Watergate secrets stirred up even more support for the bill. Nevertheless, on October 18, 1974, Ford vetoed the bill. Ford had supported the amended FOIA initially. As a congressman, he had voted for the 1966 act, and as the nation's new president, he pledged to run an "open government." But Ford's chief of staff Donald Rumsfeld, who had pushed for the original FOIA under a Democratic president, helped persuade Ford, a Republican, to veto the bill. Rumsfeld and his deputy Dick Cheney (later vice president under George W. Bush) contended that the bill was unconstitutional and expressed concerns about leaks that would harm the nation's security. The members of the Cabinet also urged Ford to veto the legislation. Antonin Scalia, a Justice Department lawyer who would later become a Supreme Court justice, asked the CIA to let Ford know of the agency's opposition, which the agency did.

The members of Congress responded by overriding Ford's veto by a huge margin. On November 20 the House voted against the presidential action, 371 to 31. During the brief debate on the bill after Ford's veto, Representative Moorhead, who had sponsored the initial bill, asked Congress to give their wholehearted support to the measure: "Let our voices here today make clear to the doubting citizens of America that Congress, at least, is committed to the principle of open government." Representative Bill Alexander, a Democrat from Arkansas, added his comments in a booming voice. "Hasn't the White House learned that Government secrecy is the real enemy of democracy?"

On the following day the Senate took similar action, rejecting the veto by a smaller, but still substantial, margin of 65 to 27. In his support of the measure, Senator Baker told colleagues, "Two recent tragedies, the war in Vietnam and Watergate, might not have occurred if executive branch officials had not been able to mask their acts in secrecy."

That same year, Moss helped pass the Privacy Act of 1974. The law, a companion to the FOIA, allows Americans to have access to their own personal records. Under the law, people can request corrections in inaccurate records. The act also protects personal information, such as financial transactions, medical data, or sexual orientation, from being released to others by the government.

How to File a

Filing a request for information under the Freedom of Information Act is as simple as writing a letter to the agency involved. Each federal agency processes requests for information under its jurisdiction. Some agencies even provide a sample letter on their website that citizens can use when requesting information. There is no central FOIA office that handles requests. Note that the FOIA does not cover records held by Congress or the federal courts. These are the steps to follow when filing a request for information from the federal government:

- Determine which agency holds the documents you want. The law requires each government department to provide an index or listing of materials and a contact person (available on the agency's website).
- In your letter, describe the record you are seeking in as much detail as possible. If the description is not sufficient, a staff member will ask you for additional information. You should provide the document's title, author, subject matter, and date if possible. You do not have to give a reason for your request.
- Agree to pay a fee of up to $25 for processing the request. You may also be charged reasonable costs for photocopying and other expenses (including staff time to search for the records). Under the law, agencies cannot charge a search fee for members of the news media, educational institutions, and noncommercial scientific use.

The law requires the agency to respond to your request within twenty business days. If the material can be released, the agency is required to make it available as soon as any applicable fee is paid. If part of the record is withheld, the

FOIA Request

Blanked-out lines in a congressional report on the U.S. terrorist attacks on September 11, 2001. Various sources reported that the secret passages referred to Saudi Arabia's role in the attacks, which that country disputed.

agency must show where the deletion occurs and how much material is missing, as long as that information does not itself fall under a FOIA exemption. In many cases, however, the agency cannot or will not respond by the deadline. Sometimes the request requires a lengthy search of thousands of pages of material. The law allows agencies to extend the deadline in "unusual circumstances," but officials must let the person making the request know of the delay in writing.

If the material you seek is not turned over, the agency must provide you with a signed letter stating the reason for the denial of your request. To be legally withheld, the records must fall within one of the nine categories stated in the FOIA. Certain personal papers relating to people other than the person making the request may be withheld if the records are covered by privacy laws. A denial may also be issued when the agency cannot find the records or they do not exist.

You may appeal a denial in writing to the department head within sixty days. If that does not resolve the matter, you may file a suit in federal district court to overturn the denial. The law requires the agency to pay legal fees and court costs if the case is ultimately decided in your favor.

PRESIDENTIAL ORDERS AND NEW AMENDMENTS
Congress approved additional amendments to the original
FOIA in 1976 and 1986. The 1976 revisions, included in the
Government in the Sunshine Act, narrowed the third FOIA
exemption (materials closed by other laws). Under the new
rules, the exemption was limited to seven categories:

- Information related to national defense.
- Internal personnel rules and operations.
- Records accusing a person of a crime.
- Documents infringing on a person's privacy.
- Records on a criminal investigation when their
release would interfere with criminal proceedings.
- Information on financial institutions when its
release would create unstable conditions or
encourage risky investments by speculators.
- Information on court proceedings that related
directly to an agency's case.

The 1986 amendments set up a new schedule of fees
charged to those requesting information under FOIA. It also
specified how to apply for a waiver of fees. But the new revisions loosened FOIA restrictions on law enforcement agencies and allowed them to withhold many more documents
than before. Two years earlier, Congress had passed the Central Intelligence Agency Information Act, which allowed the
CIA to keep additional documents under wraps.

Under presidents Ford, a Republican, and Jimmy Carter,
a Democrat, the official policy had been that agencies were
expected to comply with the FOIA and release all information not covered by exemptions. Republican President Ronald Reagan changed direction when he announced that the

Shelves at the Ronald Reagan Presidential Library in California hold 59,850 pages of documents from the Reagan administration. The documents, which had been closed to public view, were released in 2002.

Justice Department would defend in court any agency's decision to deny FOIA requests. This policy signaled to agencies that the focus had shifted from releasing as many documents as possible to withholding records whenever they could find "a substantial legal basis" to do so. In addition, Reagan made drastic cuts in agencies' FOIA budgets. With reduced staff and fewer resources dedicated to FOIA requests, many agencies quickly became swamped. Huge backlogs meant long delays for those requesting materials under the FOIA.

Even with Reagan's efforts to weaken the FOIA, the law remained a force to reckon with. Congress's findings in 1991 revealed that the FOIA had served as "a valuable means" for people to learn about their government, had led to "the disclosure of waste, fraud, abuse, and wrongdoing in the federal government," and had helped to identify "unsafe consumer products, harmful drugs, and serious health hazards."

The administration of President Bill Clinton, a Democrat, issued new marching orders to agencies in 1993. Attorney General Janet Reno ordered all federal agencies and departments to open government records to the public whenever possible. The order reversed the policy established by Reagan and continued by President George H. W. Bush. The Clinton administration said it would not defend agencies sued under the FOIA if they could not show that it was "reasonably foreseeable" that the disclosure of withheld records "would be harmful" to the nation. Clinton said he was "committed to enhancing" the act's effectiveness during his administration. Critics later questioned the president's support for openness in government, however, when he evaded questions about his affair with White House intern Monica Lewinsky. The House impeached Clinton for lying about the scandal in 1998 but the Senate acquitted him the following year.

To improve access even more, Congress passed the Electronic Freedom of Information Act Amendments of 1996 to cover computer-generated records and to make documents more accessible online. The new law requires agencies to disclose electronic files under the same rules as other records and to make records available electronically whenever possible. Before the 1996 revisions, some agencies denied access to computerized records or released mounds of printed documents instead of making the electronic version available.

"Since 1966, the world has changed a great deal," President Clinton said when he signed the 1996 amendments to the act. "Our country was founded on democratic principles of openness and accountability, and for 30 years, FOIA has supported these principles. Today, the [new law] reforges an important link between the United States government and the American people."

CHAPTER FIVE

FOIA in the Twenty-first Century

On September 11, 2001, members of an Islamic extremist group known as Al-Qaeda commandeered four U.S. passenger planes. Two planes flew into the twin towers of the World Trade Center in New York City, both of which collapsed shortly afterward. A third plane demolished a section of the Pentagon headquarters of the Defense Department in Arlington, Virginia. The fourth plane was headed toward Washington, D.C., when passengers attempted to overtake the hijackers, and the plane crashed in a field in southwestern Pennsylvania. The attacks killed nearly three thousand people, including rescue workers and passengers and crew on the planes.

Americans responded to the devastation with shock, horror, and fear. Government leaders almost immediately began planning defense measures in the wake of the worst terrorist attack in the nation's history. The day after the disaster, staff members in the Justice Department began crafting proposals for new laws designed to aid law enforcement officials in waging war on terrorism. Members of Congress worked on their own versions of antiterrorist proposals. The result of these efforts, the Uniting and Strengthening America by Providing Appropriate Tools Required to Intercept and Obstruct Terrorism Act (USA Patriot Act), passed a nearly unanimous Congress, and on October 26, 2001, President George W. Bush signed the legislation into law. Among other things, the act gave law enforcement more powers and the American public fewer rights to challenge secrecy and obtain information on government operations. Under the law, the government could detain people secretly without going through the court system or making arrest records public. In 2002 Congress passed the Homeland Security Act, which set up a new department to handle terrorism and national security.

With the passage of the Patriot Act and the Homeland Security Act, the national focus shifted toward national security and away from personal liberties. Supporters of the new laws believed that such a shift was necessary to fight terrorism and prevent future attacks. Critics, however, believed that government officials had abused such power in the past and would be even more likely to take advantage of their position with the safeguards removed by the Patriot Act. Because both the Patriot Act and the Homeland Security Act focus on national security, the public cannot oversee their administration. Most, if not all, of the information collected and dispersed under the new laws—including documents in the Justice Department and the Federal Bureau of Investigation—is exempt from the Freedom of Information Act. Even members of Congress are barred from seeing much of the material.

The Senate Judiciary Committee's 2003 report on the FBI

highlighted the importance of Congress's oversight of government operations—and the need for public information. "Public scrutiny and debate regarding the actions of governmental agencies as powerful as the DOJ [Department of Justice] and the FBI are critical to explaining actions to the citizens to whom these agencies are ultimately accountable. In this way, congressional oversight plays a critical role in our democracy."

Senator Russell Feingold, a Wisconsin Democrat and the only member of the Senate to vote against the Patriot Act, warned against the erosion of personal liberties in the heat of anti-terrorist fervor. "We must continue to respect our Constitution and protect our civil liberties in the wake of the attacks," Feingold declared after passage of the law. "Congress will fulfill its duty only when it protects both the American people and the freedoms at the foundation of American society."

SECRECY AT A "NEW LEVEL"

Many government officials and agencies reacted to the fears of further terrorist attacks by sealing documents previously open to the public. Even before 9/11, President George W. Bush's administration took measures to tighten secrecy around government operations. The Bush administration closed some court proceedings, increased the number of classified documents (up 18 percent between October 2000 and September 2001), and sought to keep secret the details of Vice President Dick Cheney's energy task force. While many presidents had tried to keep their records private, Bush took secrecy "to a new level," said historian Alan Brinkley. Dozens of experts said the policies of the Bush administration represented "a sea change in government openness," according to a report in the *New York Times*.

One month after the attack on the World Trade Center and the Pentagon, Attorney General John Ashcroft moved to quash requests for government information whenever possible. Ashcroft issued a memorandum to all federal departments and agencies to "carefully consider" requests made under the FOIA and to consult with the Department of Justice about any "significant FOIA issues." In carefully phrased terms, Ashcroft basically encouraged department heads to keep documents secret if they could by first considering all the exemptions allowed under the law and to grant access only when absolutely required.

"Any discretionary decision by your agency to disclose information protected under the FOIA should be made only after full and deliberate consideration of the institutional, commercial, and personal privacy interests that could be implicated by disclosure of the information," the memo instructed. Ashcroft pledged that the Justice Department would defend any agency head who withheld records. The Ashcroft memorandum reversed Reno's directive for an open-government policy issued in 1993. The edict outraged many Americans, who believed the order was a direct assault on the people's right to know.

The following March District Court Judge Gladys Kessler chastised the Energy Department for its "glacial pace" in filling requests for information under the FOIA. "The government can offer no legal or practical excuse for its excessive delay," the judge wrote in ordering the release of documents connected to Vice President Cheney's energy task force. In 2003, two years after the Ashcroft memorandum had been issued, the General Accounting Office reported that about one-third of agency heads said they were less likely to release information after the memo was issued.

Dick Cheney holds secret documents on June 12, 1990, when he was secretary of defense. Cheney later served as vice president under George W. Bush. In that post, Cheney resisted attempts to force him to release documents related to his energy task force.

An official of the James Madison Project, a private organization devoted to open government, said Ashcroft's order put "the fear of God" in officials responsible for responding to FOIA requests. It served as an "informal threat that secrecy should reign . . . because your job is on the line." PBS commentator Bill Moyers, who as press secretary helped persuade President Lyndon Johnson to sign the original FOIA, noted that the Ashcroft order affected far more than records related to national defense. Bush's policies, he said, denied access to government records to historians, members of the press, Congress, and the public.

"Keeping us from finding out about the possibility of accidents at chemical plants is not about national security; it's about covering up an industry's indiscretions," Moyers said. "Locking up the secrets of . . . meetings with energy executives is not about national security; it's about hiding the confidential memorandum sent to the White House by Exxon Mobil showing the influence of oil companies on the administration's policy on global warming." The Exxon memorandum, unearthed despite White House efforts to withhold the records of Cheney's energy task force, came to light through a reporter's request for the document under the Freedom of Information Act.

In addition to the Ashcroft memorandum, agencies received orders from White House Chief of Staff Andrew H. Card Jr. to deny access to "sensitive but unclassified" documents. Shortly after the 9/11 tragedy, the National Archives and Records Administration reclassified more than 1.1 million pages of documents to hide them from public view. The director later acknowledged that at least one-third of the material should have remained accessible. Most state governments have also considered tightening their freedom of information laws. A survey of state legislatures by the University of Missouri's Freedom of Information Center revealed that at least twenty states have discussed revisions in their open government laws since the 9/11 attacks.

President Bush, like others before him, also relied on executive privilege to keep documents secret from the public and Congress. In November 2001 Bush issued an executive order to delay the release of the presidential papers of Ronald Reagan and future presidents. Congressman Douglas Ose, a

California Republican, said the order "undercuts the public's right to be fully informed about how its government operated in the past. It is an affront to the citizens of this country." An effort by Congress to pass a law to override Bush's order failed. However, Barack Obama lifted the order when he became president in 2009.

In December 2001 President Bush refused to turn over FBI records subpoenaed by Congress during an investigation into FBI ties to the Mafia in South Boston. The refusal angered many, including Representative Dan Burton, chairman of the House Committee on Government Reform and a conservative Republican who had attacked Democratic president Bill Clinton for keeping secrets. "I believe a veil of secrecy has descended around the administration," Burton said. He suggested that the Justice Department was "more interested in creating a new policy of secrecy than in accommodating our need to get to the bottom of the Boston mess."

PATRIOTIC SECRETS OR DANGEROUS COVER-UPS?

Since most citizens lack the resources, knowledge, and time to conduct their own investigations into governmental misbehavior, they rely on Congress, the press, and public interest groups to uncover questionable actions and programs. Often these investigations bump up against the FOIA's exemption for documents that are hidden to protect the nation's security. Proving whether information does or does not qualify for the national security exemption is among the greatest challenges of the FOIA. In some instances, different agencies have disagreed on whether certain documents should or should not remain secret. When a FOIA request is denied, a petitioner can take the case to court, and under the current law a judge may review the disputed documents in private to determine whether they should be kept secret or made public. The answer to that question is not always clear-cut. In some cases there is no doubt that the documents do not qualify for an exemption. But in other cases, there are valid arguments on both sides of the issue. Sometimes it boils down to a difference of interpretation. The FOIA, however, requires government agencies to back up their claims with facts whenever they turn down a request for documents.

In Erwin, Tennessee, for example, officials at a nuclear fuel processing plant kept secret several serious accidents inside the facility, including a uranium spill that could have led to a deadly nuclear reaction. The Nuclear Regulatory Commission (NRC) removed reports on the accidents from its public archives in 2004 because of concerns that terrorists would use the information to exploit the situation. The NRC and citizens disagreed, however, over whether the terrorists or the conditions at the plant posed the greater danger.

Neighbors and workers at the plant never learned of the spill and other safety violations over a three-year period. The press finally broke the story after the NRC issued an order requiring the plant to make improvements. The "three-year veil of secrecy," the media's term for the blackout, drew howls of protests from critics. "What rationale can be divined," news editor Thomas Mitchell asked, "that would argue for keeping serious accidents inside the plant from some hypothetical enemy, foreign or domestic? Unless, of course, the 'enemy' are nearby residents who might've become a bit alarmed at the prospect of an 'uncontrolled nuclear reaction.'"

In another case, several newspapers, including the *New York Times* and the *Wall Street Journal,* published articles in June 2006 on the Bush administration's hiring of a Belgian firm to track the financial dealings of suspected terrorists.

President Bush said that the deal should have remained secret and chastised the newspapers for the "disgraceful" act of printing an article that put the nation at risk.

While several readers applauded the decision to publish the story, others feared that it undermined U.S. efforts to root out terrorists. A World War II veteran said that alerting terrorists to the financial trackers had the same effect that releasing secret military codes to the enemy would have had during the 1940s. Another critic charged that the newspapers that published the story had "done a serious disservice to our country" by warning terrorists to avoid certain financial transactions.

Media commentator Tom Brokaw presented the opposite view. He noted that the basic story—that terrorists' financial dealings were being tracked—was already a matter of public knowledge. "I don't know anyone who believes that the terrorist network said, 'Oh my God, they're tracing our financial transactions? What a surprise.' Of course, they knew that they were doing that," Brokaw said.

A TOUGH NEW BILL

In 2007 the National Security Archive, a research group at George Washington University dedicated to open government, reported that some FOIA requests for information had languished for more than fifteen years in the files of the State Department, the CIA, the FBI, the Justice Department, and the Air Force. Twelve agencies, including the Environmental Protection Agency and the Defense Department, had delayed requests for ten years or more. Not only the public, businesses, and the news media were stymied by the informational roadblocks; members of Congress also had to fight their own battles to unearth government records. Blocked from getting the information they believed essential to do their job, members of Congress renewed efforts to pass amendments to strengthen the FOIA. Politicians from both political parties, the media, public interest groups, and members of the public all protested the barriers erected by the Bush administration. Republican Senator Charles E. Grassley of Iowa said it was becoming harder to get information and that he was "running into more and more stonewalls" when requesting materials from executive branch agencies. Democrat Patrick J. Leahy from Vermont, a member of the Senate since 1974, said he had "never known an administration that is more difficult to get information from."

On March 5, 2007, Representative William Clay, a Democrat from Missouri, introduced the Freedom of Information Act Amendments in the House. A similar bill, the OPEN (Openness Promotes Effectiveness in our National) Government Act, introduced by Senators Leahy and John Cornyn, a Republican from Texas, went before the Senate on March 13. The measures won support from a broad range of organizations—from the conservative Heritage Foundation to the business-oriented U.S. Chamber of Commerce to the liberal American Civil Liberties Union. The legislation to amend the FOIA called for "accessibility, accountability, and openness" in the federal government. It strengthened the FOIA and provided tools to get information from agencies more quickly.

The House passed its version of the bill by a wide margin (308 to 117) on March 14 with little debate, but action on the measure came to a standstill in the Senate. Despite a unanimous recommendation by the Senate's Judiciary Committee that the legislation should pass, an unnamed senator put a "secret hold" on the legislation. A Senate custom allows any member of that body to block a bill from being debated by

Senator Patrick J. Leahy (*center*) confers with Representative Todd Platts (*left*) and Senator John Cornyn (*right*) before a hearing on the Freedom of Information Act. Leahy and Cornyn sponsored a bill to toughen the FOIA.

the full Senate by secretly objecting to it. Observers noted the irony of a bill to control government secrecy being stopped by an anonymous senator, acting behind closed doors.

The Society of Professional Journalists unveiled the secret senator as Jon Kyl, an Arizona Republican, who put the hold in place because of Justice Department objections to the bill. Senator Kyl dropped his objection when senators made some changes in the bill, and on August 3, 2007, the Senate passed the measure by unanimous consent.

After months of negotiations between Senate and House members, a compromise bill won the unanimous consent of

the Senate on December 14, 2007, the same day it was introduced. Members of the House passed, by voice vote, an identical version of the act four days later. The final bill:

- set up a hotline for citizens to call to track progress on their requests.
- provided for an ombudsman and set up a new
office, the Office of Government Information Services, to review FOIA operations, advise on changes
needed in the system, and mediate disputes.
- required agencies to disclose which exemption
applies when withholding information.
- levied penalties against agencies that take more
than twenty days to deal with FOIA requests. Under
the law, agencies that release information after the
deadline could no longer charge for research or
copying expenses.
- awarded court and legal fees to those who win
their FOIA cases in court or who are allowed to see
requested documents after an agency reverses its
decision to withhold records once a lawsuit is filed.
- required agencies who lose FOIA cases to pay
court and attorney fees. Previously the fees came
from the U.S. Treasury.
- required the Special Counsel to investigate
agency officials who lose FOIA cases to determine
if they should be disciplined for not complying
with the law.
- called for an annual report to Congress on FOIA
cases and resultant disciplinary actions.
- specified that FOIA requirements apply to private contractors working on government projects.

On December 31, 2007, under pressure from Republican members of Congress, a reluctant President Bush signed the bill into law. The president also signed an accompanying bill that required the White House budget office to post information about government contracts on line. The bill, introduced by then–Senator Barack Obama and Senator Tom Coburn, Republican from Oklahoma, received support from members of both parties.

Commenting on the new open-government laws, Republican Senator Susan Collins of Maine said that the administration had "brought these challenges on itself." A powerful member of the Senate Homeland Security and Governmental Affairs Committee, Collins joined other Republicans in supporting the FOIA amendments. "By trying to keep secret information that doesn't need to be secret," Collins said, "[the administration] invites skepticism of all of its secrecy claims."

EFFECT ON BUSINESS AND SCIENCE

Each year government agencies receive more than one million requests for information under the FOIA. Of those, an estimated 60 percent are filed by businesses. Citizens form the second-largest group seeking information under the law, while organizations such as the Society for the Prevention of Cruelty to Animals, Consumers Union, and the Michigan Republican Party, file around 3 percent of the requests for records. Journalists make only about 6 percent of the FOIA requests.

Companies use the FOIA to collect all kinds of information that helps their business: government forecasts on the economy, sales trends, reports on industry, economic data, information on government projects and grants, competitors' bids and products, and detailed weather analyses.

Some businesses use the services of data brokers who collect government information on a variety of topics for their clients. Lawyers are increasingly using information obtained through the FOIA to defend clients facing insider trading charges and other cases involving government agencies. Attorneys also rely on the FOIA to gather information in lawsuits against government agencies, businesses, and private individuals.

While many firms rely on information collected under the FOIA, the law has its detractors among business leaders. Some company executives claim that the FOIA allows competitors to steal insider information. The access to private business records provided by the FOIA, they say, gives competitors an unfair advantage, reduces the amount companies can earn from their inventions, and undercuts the spirit of entrepreneurship.

Since many large firms depend on government funds for at least part of their research and development costs, a significant number of corporations fall under FOIA rules that require data paid for with federal money be opened to the public. Existing laws protect trade secrets and patents, but other relevant research material can be gathered through the FOIA process. Such material, say some business leaders, may help other firms duplicate products or processes that the original company has created. If that happens, the company may receive less for its product than it would have otherwise. This reduction in market value may discourage companies from investing in research and development in the future, company executives say. Without the lure of big profits, companies may delay or never discover innovations that could benefit Americans' lives.

A ruling issued by the District of Columbia circuit court in

Critical Mass Energy Project v. *NRC* in 1992 has reduced the amount of business information released under the FOIA. The court ruled that businesses that voluntarily provide the government with certain data can ask that the information be kept secret if the company would not normally make the material public itself. While many of the nation's courts have followed the D.C. court's ruling, California's federal district court and others around the country have not. The U.S. Supreme Court has not yet ruled on the matter.

People outside the business world have criticized the heavy use of the FOIA by corporations. They complain that the constant requests put a heavy financial burden on agencies and that businesses should pay more of the cost of processing the materials requested. In a few cases, corporations have used the FOIA to harass agencies whose policies they dislike.

In the late 1980s and early 1990s, for example, tobacco companies and smokers' rights groups inundated California state and local agencies with requests for information after the state launched an aggressive antismoking campaign. The National Cancer Institute (NCI) used records obtained through the FOIA to document the tobacco companies' actions during this time.

The NCI study found that the tobacco firms targeted agencies involved in the campaign to reduce cigarette use. The strategy put a strain on the agencies' budgets and staff time. The tobacco companies used the documents they gathered to learn how the agencies operated, information they utilized when devising counterattacks against the antismoking campaigns. Tobacco company advertisements aimed to discredit the federal programs as a waste of taxpayers' money.

Once they realized what the companies were doing, the California agencies took longer to fill the FOIA requests and followed other procedures more stringently than they normally would have. These tactics eventually ended the tobacco firms' onslaught of FOIA requests.

In the scientific world, secrecy is often seen as an impediment to scientific progress. "Secrecy and nationalism . . . discourage the sharing of knowledge that is so crucial to scientific progress, and they hamper global competitiveness, a necessary component of the great march forward," the editors of *Science* magazine stated in an editorial on secrecy.

Other commentators who support openness note that science has the potential to cause great harm with its inventions (from nuclear bombs to insecticides). The public and Congress need access to technical information, they say, in order to control scientific advances and prevent disaster. Since its founding sixty years ago by nuclear scientists, the Federation of American Scientists has promoted public access to government records. The national group uncovers and publishes government documents on controversial issues and provides Congress with nontechnical analyses of nuclear and other scientific matters. "Restrictions on access to information are a perennial problem in national security policy," the group observed in its 2007 annual report.

Nevertheless, there are legitimate reasons to limit the release of scientific data and to control when the information is made available to the public. The FOIA protects trade secrets and commercial interests as well as research conducted on secret weapons systems and other projects that genuinely fall under the national security exemption.

Bruce Alberts, president of the National Academy of Sciences, told Congress in 1999 that it would take too much time and money to make available all scientific information in which the federal government played a role. "Valuable

Open Government = Big Business

When Congress enacted the FOIA in 1966, most observers expected members of the news media to jam the doors of federal agencies in search of information. As it turned out, businesses are the ones standing in line to see government records. Corporations file ten times as many FOIA requests as members of the news media do. Law firms, the most frequent FOIA petitioners, account for about 25 percent of all requests. Commercial data brokers have made a business for themselves out of FOIA requests, procuring FOIA information and reselling it to corporations. They make the second-highest number of requests, filing more than 12 percent of the FOIA petitions for information.

The heavy use of the FOIA by businesses is an indication of how much capitalism depends on the free flow of information. The Freedom of Information Act serves as a door to business information, research data and results, surveys, polls, details on government projects, weather reports and forecasts, and much more. Businesses use the information they gain through FOIA requests in a multitude of ways. Among the requests for FOIA from businesses, law firms, and commercial users in 2006:

- the amount of asbestos on decommissioned Navy ships;
- cockpit readings for airliners involved in a crash;
- background information on prospective employees;
- research for a movie on Guantanamo;
- information on the whereabouts of parents owing child support payments;
- material on unions used by companies trying to avoid unionization.

resources will be deflected from science into FOIA related administration, bookkeeping and legal battles," he said.

Alberts also argued against releasing data prematurely, which would allow commercial firms to use universities' research for their own gain. Foreign countries would also have access to research projects still being developed by U.S. firms. Researchers would have no time for careful analysis in their rush to publish their work before competitors reported on released data. Alberts expressed concern that a completely open policy toward research could expose the identity of people participating in tests. Such revelations could deter people from volunteering for research projects.

STATE AND INTERNATIONAL EFFORTS

When President Lyndon B. Johnson signed the Freedom of Information Act in 1966, the United States became only the fifth nation in the world to enact a federal law that required public access to government information. Sweden passed the first Freedom of Information Act in 1766. The law, an integral part of the country's constitution, guaranteed freedom of the press and the right of every Swedish citizen to "free access to official documents, in order to encourage the free exchange of opinion."

Originally part of Sweden, Finland came under the provisions of the Swedish 1766 information act. In 1951 an independent Finland adopted its own freedom of information law, which was upgraded in 1999. Denmark adopted an information act in 1964 that allowed "any person" to demand to see documents involved in "public administration."

In South America, Colombia's 1888 Code of Political and Municipal Organization permitted people to see government documents unless other laws barred their release. The right was retained in the country's 1985 law on the publicity of official acts and documents.

By 2006 sixty-eight countries had adopted public access laws, with many enacted in the previous decade. Another fifty were considering such laws, and at least eighty nations had adopted provisions in their constitutions to allow a right of access to information. Many international treaties, pacts, and other agreements have included passages guaranteeing the right of the public to examine public documents. International groups have also recognized the freedom to view public information as a human right.

Although the growing international support for freedom of information is encouraging, more remains to be done in the campaign for access. Some freedom of information laws apply only to personal data; others are limited to information about the environment or other topics. "The culture of secrecy remains strong in many countries," writes David Banisar, who conducted the global survey of freedom of information statutes. Several of the freedom of information laws "promote access in name only." Some countries block access with high fees or cumbersome regulations. Others exempt too much material from public view. Still others have not adopted new technologies, like computer access, to make it easier to view documents. Banisar says the global war on terrorism has led to new laws that promote secrecy and prevent access to public documents.

All states and the District of Columbia have freedom of information laws on the books, though some are stronger than others. Vermont's law, among the broadest, covers the records of all government entities, including town boards and commissions. Anyone can request to see public records for whatever reason (or no reason). Information exempted from public view includes personal records such as tax returns (but not lists of taxpayers), trade secrets, records on criminal investigations, and documents protected by other laws. The state law has no specific exemption for homeland security, but it does allow officials to withhold information whose disclosure would threaten people's safety or "the security of public property."

On the other end of the spectrum, the law governing access to information in the District of Columbia is among the most restrictive. While the federal law and those of many states exempt personnel, medical, and similar information from public disclosure, the District of Columbia keeps secret all information "of a personal nature," when disclosure would be an "unwarranted invasion of privacy." The D.C. law includes several other exemptions that relate to information on local antitrust investigations, arson cases, and vital records such as birth and death certificates, marriage and divorce papers, and other personal data.

BENEFITS OF AN OPEN POLICY

In a democracy the most important benefit of freedom of information laws is that they give citizens the knowledge they need to be active, valuable participants in the democratic process. But Banisar sees many other benefits to allowing the public to have access to government records. Among them:

> • People who know the reasons behind government decisions are more likely to support the laws and actions that result. Information can dispel misunderstandings and dissatisfaction. People feel included in the decision-making process.

- An informed public (and Congress) can oversee government operations more effectively. Armed with information, they can check on government performance and shine a spotlight on graft and incompetence.
- People's confidence in government increases when they can learn for themselves what officials are doing.
- The prospect of open records improves the performance of government bodies. Officials who know the public has access to their records are more likely to base decisions on objective facts that can justify their actions.
- Access to information can help preserve other rights. Advocates have used government records to bring to light instances of human rights abuses, such as the use of torture and illegal wiretapping. Proponents of economic justice have used public records to show mishandling of aid programs and unequal treatment of loan and grant applicants.
- Open books can help protect against government fraud and corruption. Public officials must be able to justify the awarding of contracts and other business deals.
- Government documents can provide a way to redress past wrongs. American Indians, for example, used old treaty agreements to press their case for fair treatment in court.

A TRANSPARENT TOMORROW?

When presidents and officials are allowed to keep the public's business secret, there is no way for Congress or citizens to check for graft, inefficiencies, or abuse of power. "The constitutional health of our democracy depends on transparency," writes Emily Berman, a lawyer with the Brennan Center for Justice, a progressive, nonpartisan institute at New York University School of Law formed as a tribute to Justice William Brennan and focused on issues of democracy and justice. Banisar agrees: "The public is only truly able to participate in the democratic process," he says, "when they have information about the activities and policies of the government."

Quinlan J. Shea Jr., former director of the Justice Department's Office of Privacy and Information Appeals, notes that the FOIA "helps us to learn what is actually going on inside our government. I have long believed that secrecy is the mortal enemy of democracy. The more secrecy, the less democracy. The more that citizens are told that they must trust their government—that they must take on faith its integrity, and the value of what the government is doing and why it is doing it—the greater is the tendency away from democracy as we would like to see it."

During his campaign for president in 2008, Democrat Barack Obama promised to follow an open-government policy. On his first full day in office, President Obama reversed the Ashcroft memorandum encouraging federal agencies to keep secrets. In a memorandum of his own, he ordered all executive branch officials to run their departments under the principles of openness and transparency.

In his memo, Obama stated: "The Freedom of Information Act should be administered with a clear presumption: In the face of doubt, openness prevails. The Government should not keep information confidential merely because public officials might be embarrassed by disclosure, because errors and failures might be revealed, or because of speculative or abstract

As a presidential candidate in 2008, Senator Barack Obama pledged to adopt an open-government policy that guaranteed Americans access to official documents. During his first days in office, President Obama ordered federal agencies to operate as openly as possible, but critics have charged that other actions by the president have undercut citizens' right to information about their government.

fears." In addition Obama appointed a three-person board to develop guidelines for agencies to follow to accomplish those principles. The president instructed the attorney general to operate in the same spirit of openness. He also included himself in the new policy, pledging to check with the attorney general and the White House counsel before invoking executive privilege.

"For a long time now, there's been too much secrecy in this city," Obama told staff members and Cabinet secretaries.

"The Freedom of Information Act is perhaps the most powerful instrument we have for making our government honest and transparent, and of holding it accountable. And I expect members of my administration not simply to live up to the letter but also the spirit of this law." While acknowledging that the memorandum would not transform the government overnight, he noted, "These historic measures do mark the beginning of a new era of openness in our country."

In addition, the Obama administration posted a list of official visitors to the White House on the Internet for the first time ever, set up a blog for Americans to submit suggestions on declassifying material, posted other government records online, and promised to open sensitive but unclassified information to the public. Obama adopted some of the public's advice when he issued an executive order in December 2009 pledging to allow public access to material that is declassified. He also made a commitment to speed up the process by declassifying 100 million pages of government records a year. In a year's time the number of old unresolved FOIA requests fell from 124,019 to 67,764, a review conducted by the Associated Press (AP) in 2009 found. The Justice Department under Obama has reported a 5 percent increase in the number of cases where a request for information has been completely fulfilled.

While advocates of the FOIA have applauded Obama's open-government positions, they have questioned whether his actions will match his words. Delays still hamper efforts to obtain information from government agencies. During Obama's first year as president, those requesting to see government records filed more than three hundred FOIA lawsuits after agencies refused to turn over records. The AP review reported that seventeen major federal agencies declined FOIA requests at least 466,872 times in fiscal year 2009, which included nine months during which Obama was president. The number of FOIA denials was up from 312,683 issued the year before.

Christine Erickson, of the Public Employees for Environmental Responsibility, whose FOIA request was denied, said she finds it frustrating that agencies are still forcing people to go to court because "they are afraid that releasing the information will be embarrassing" to the agency.

In February 2009 Obama directed the Justice Department to push the courts to drop a case involving five foreigners who claim they were secretly jailed, interrogated, and tortured under the CIA's "extraordinary rendition" program. Like George W. Bush, Obama claimed that a trial would endanger national security. "The Justice Department will ensure the [state secrets] privilege is not invoked to hide from the American people information about their government's actions that they have a right to know," Justice Department spokesman Matt Miller pledged. "This administration will be transparent and open, consistent with our national security obligations."

The assurance did little to quell the outrage of Anthony D. Romero, executive director of the American Civil Liberties Union, which filed the case for the men. "[Attorney General] Eric Holder . . . stood up in court today and said that [the Justice Department] would continue the Bush policy of invoking state secrets to hide the reprehensible history of torture, rendition and the most grievous human rights violations committed by the American government. This is not change. This is definitely more of the same."

Like other presidents before him, Obama has resisted calls from Congress to have his staff testify. After a breach in security at a White House dinner party in 2009, some members of Congress suggested Obama's social secretary should discuss the matter with them. In response, press secretary Robert Gibbs told reporters, "Based on the separation of powers, staff here don't go to testify in front of Congress." Obama's reliance on the separation of powers and executive privilege did not sit well with open-government advocates. "It doesn't even pass the laugh test," said Mark Rozell, professor of public policy at George Mason University. "This definitely goes against the president's own pledge for a more open administration, and to move beyond the secrecy practices of the Bush era."

A year after issuing the FOIA memorandum, Obama acknowledged that much work remained to be done to open government to public scrutiny. An audit conducted by the National Security Archive found that only thirteen of ninety agencies had taken concrete steps to reform the FOIA process in their offices. The report, released in March 2010, noted that several agencies still had backlogs going back as much as eighteen years. "The Obama administration deserves an A for effort," said Tom Blanton, director of the National Security Archive, "but an Incomplete for results. It's too soon for a final judgment . . . most agencies [have] yet to walk the walk."

The Obama administration responded by issuing a new memorandum, this one from Chief of Staff Rahm Emanuel, directing agencies to take specific steps to implement FOIA reforms. These included updating training materials and instruction manuals and devoting adequate time and money to meet FOIA requests "promptly and cooperatively."

In 1958 Congressman John E. Moss received the John Peter Zenger Award for his work to open government records to the public. He was the first nonjournalist to receive the honor.

During his acceptance speech, Moss told reporters gathered for the occasion, "The government should not hide the facts from the American public . . . we have a right to know the truth." The "father of the Freedom of Information Act" knew well that the battle against government secrets had just begun and that it would never end. Every new election and agency reorganization brings to power men and women who need to be instructed in the importance of freedom of information. And if they do not learn the lesson on their own, then it takes an army of citizens, members of Congress, businesses, reporters, and public-service organizations—equipped with the tools provided by the Freedom of Information Act that Moss worked so hard to enact—to teach them. As veteran journalist Bill Moyers notes, "It's always a fight to find out what the government doesn't want us to know."

From Bill to Law

For a proposal to become a federal law, it must go through many steps:

In Congress:

1. A bill is proposed by a citizen, a legislator, the president, or another interested party. Most bills originate in the House and then are considered in the Senate.

2. A representative submits the bill to the House (the first reading). A senator submits it to the Senate. The person (or people) who introduces the bill is its main sponsor. Other lawmakers can become sponsors to show support for the bill. Each bill is read three times before the House or the Senate.

3. The bill is assigned a number and referred to the committee(s) and subcommittee(s) dealing with the topic. Each committee adopts its own rules, following guidelines of the House and the Senate. The committee chair controls scheduling for the bill.

4. The committees hold hearings if the bill is controversial or complex. Experts and members of the public may testify. Congress may compel witnesses to testify if they do not do so voluntarily.

5. The committee reviews the bill, discusses it, adds amendments, and makes other changes it deems necessary during markup sessions.

6. The committee votes on whether to support the bill, oppose it, or take no action on it and issues a report on its findings and recommendations.

7. A bill that receives a favorable committee report goes to the Rules Committee to be scheduled for consideration by the full House or Senate.

8. If the committee delays a bill or if the Rules Committee fails to schedule it, House members can sign a discharge motion and call for a vote on the matter. If a majority votes to release the bill from committee, it is scheduled on the calendar as any other bill would be. Senators may vote to discharge the bill from a committee as well. More commonly, though, a senator will add the bill as an amendment to an unrelated bill in order to get it past the committee blocking it. Or a senator can request that a bill be put directly on the Senate calendar, where it will be scheduled for debate. House and Senate members can also vote to suspend the rules and vote directly on a bill. Bills passed in this way must receive support from two thirds of those voting.

9. Members of both houses debate the bill. In the House, a chairperson moderates the discussion and each speaker's time is limited. Senators can speak on the issue for as long as they wish. Senators who want to block the bill may debate for hours in a tactic known as a filibuster. A three-fifths vote of the Senate is required to stop the filibuster (cloture), and talk on the bill is then limited to one hour per senator.

10. Following the debate, the bill is read section by section (the second reading). Members may propose amendments, which are voted on before the final bill comes up for a vote.

11. The full House and Senate then debate the entire bill and those amendments approved previously. Debate continues until a majority of members vote to "move the previous question" or approve a special resolution forcing a vote.

12. A full quorum—at least 218 members in the House, 51 in the Senate—must be present for a vote to be held. A member may request a formal count of members to ensure a quorum is on hand. Absent members are sought when there is no quorum.

13. Before final passage, opponents are given a last chance to propose amendments that alter the bill; the members vote on them.

14. A bill needs approval from a majority of those voting to pass. Members who do not want to take a stand on the issue may choose to abstain (not vote at all) or merely vote present.

15. If the House passes the bill, it goes on to the Senate. By that time, bills often have more than one hundred amendments attached to them. Occasionally, a Senate bill will go to the House.

16. If the bill passes in the same form in both the House and the Senate, it is sent to the clerk to be recorded.

17. If the Senate and the House version differ, the Senate sends the bill to the House with the request that members approve the changes.

18. If the two houses disagree on the changes, the bill may go to conference, where members appointed by the House and the Senate work out a compromise if possible.

19. The House and the Senate vote on the revised bill agreed to in conference. Further amendments may be added and the process repeated if the Senate and the House version of the bill differ.

20. The bill goes to the president for a signature.

To the President:

1. If the president signs the bill, it becomes law.

2. If the president vetoes the bill, it goes back to Congress, which can override his veto with a two-thirds vote in both houses.

3. If the president takes no action, the bill automatically becomes law after ten days if Congress is still in session.

4. If Congress adjourns and the president has taken no action on the bill within ten days, it does not become law. This is known as a pocket veto.

The time from introduction of the bill to the signing can range from several months to the entire two-year session. If a bill does not win approval during the session, it can be reintroduced in the next Congress, where it will have to go through the whole process again.

Notes

Introduction

p. 9, "Only the courage . . .": Bill Moyers, "Politics and Economy: Bill Moyers on the Freedom of Information Act," *Bill Moyers' Journal*, PBS, April 5, 2002. www.pbs.org/now/commentary/moyers4.html

p. 10, "a historic victory . . .": William M. Blair, "Information Bill Sent to Johnson," *New York Times*, June 21, 1966, 21.

Chapter One

p. 12, "Great inconvenience may. . .": James Breig, "Early American Newspapering," *CW Journal*, Spring 2003. www.history.org/foundation/journal/spring03/journalism.cfm

p. 12, "The debate got heated . . .": William L. Casey Jr., John E. Marthinsen, and Laurence S. Moss, *Entrepreneurship, Productivity, and the Freedom of Information Act.* Lexington, MA: Lexington Books, 1983, 11.

p. 13, "No pamphlet, . . .": Robert G. Ingersoll, *The Works of Robert G. Ingersoll*, New York: Dresden Publishing Co., 1909, 324.

p. 15, "The dialogue contained . . .": David M. O'Brien, *The Public's Right to Know: The Supreme Court and the First Amendment.* New York: Praeger Publishers, 1981, 37–38.

p. 15, "I am sorry . . .": Thomas Jefferson, "Amending the Constitution," Thomas Jefferson on Politics & Government, http://etext.virginia.edu/jefferson/quotations/jeff1000.htm. Cited in Casey Jr. et al., *Entrepreneurship, Productivity, and the Freedom of Information Act*, 5–7.

p. 16, "'Liberty,' he wrote, . . .": John Adams, "A Dissertation on the Canon and Feudal Law," 1765. Published on Teaching American History. org, Ashland, OH: Ashbrook Center for Public Affairs, Ashland University, 2006-2008. http://teachingamericanhistory.org/library/index. asp?document=43

p. 17, "The people have . . .": "Madison Debates," August 11, 1787. Published by The Avalon Project, Yale Law School,New Haven, CT: 2008. http://avalon.law.yale.edu/18th_century/debates_811.asp

p. 17, "The phrase . . .": William Wirt Henry, *Patrick Henry: Life, Correspondence and Speeches*, vol. 3, New York: Charles Scribner's Sons, 1891, 496.

p. 23, "theory that . . .": Senate Subcommittee on Administrative Practice and Procedure, "Freedom of Information Act Source Book: Legislative Materials, Cases, Articles," Washington, DC: U.S. Government Printing

Office, 1974, 6. www.llsdc.org/attachments/files/184/FOIA-LH.pdf

p. 24, "Attorney General Tom Clark, . . .": Tom C. Clark, "Attorney General's Manual on the Administrative Procedure Act, 1947," ABA Administrative Procedure DataBase. www.law.fsu.edu/library/admin/1947ii.html

p. 25, "It is desired . . .": O. G. Haywood Jr., "Note to Dr. Fidler from O. G. Haywood, Jr. on Medical Experiments on Humans, April 17, 1947," Department of Energy, www.hss.energy.gov/healthsafety/ohre/road map/overview/074930/index.html

p. 25, "Senators working . . .": Senate Committee on the Judiciary, "Clarifying and Protecting the Right of the Public to Information and for Other Purposes," Senate Report No. 1219, 88th Cong., 2nd Session, July 22, 1964.

p. 30, "You can't just simply . . .": Norman Hillmer, "The Canadian Caper," The Canadian Encyclopedia. Historica Foundation of Canada, 2010. http://thecanadianencyclopedia.com/PrinterFriendly.cfm?Params =A1ARTFET_E74

p. 30, "Photos of American . . .": Pat Arnow, "From Self-Censorship to Official Censorship," FAIR: Fairness & Accuracy In Reporting, March/April 2007, www.fair.org/index.php?page=3095

p. 31, "Kent Cooper, . . .": Editorial, "The People's Right to Know: How Much or How Little?" Time magazine, January 11, 1971, www.time.com/time/magazine/article/0,9171,876841,00.html

Chapter Two

p. 33, "rights of newspapers . . .": Paul Alfred Pratte, Gods Within the Machine: A History of the American Society of Newspapers, Westport, CT: Praeger Publishers, 1995, 90–91.

p. 33, "most vital . . .": Harold L. Cross, The People's Right to Know: Legal Access to Public Records and Proceedings. New York: Columbia University Press, 1953, 4.

p. 34, "The right to speak . . .": John W. Beckler and Bem Price, "Fight Against Secrecy Nears End," Arizona Republic, June 12, 1966, 16B.

p. 34, "welter of . . .": Cross, The People's Right to Know, 4.

p. 35, "The records . . .": Cross, The People's Right to Know, 10.

p. 36, "Cross concluded . . .": Cross, The People's Right to Know, 246.

p. 37, "There is a state . . .": Allen Drury, "U.S. Suppression of News Charged," New York Times, November 8, 1955, 25.

p. 37, "In further testimony . . .": Drury, "U.S. Suppression of News Charged."

p. 39, "silly cover-up . . .": Michael Doyle, "Right-to-know crusader Moss was FBI's thorn," Sacramento Bee, September 2, 2001, www.johnemoss foundation.org/capalert05.htm

p. 39, "full explanation . . .": "News Secrecy Decried: House Member Raises

Issue Over Mouse in Rocket," *New York Times*, May 4, 1958, 6.

p. 40, "one of the greatest . . .": Ward Sinclair, "The Man Who Perfected Oversight," *Washington Post*, January 14, 1979, www.johnemossfounda tion.org/sinclair.htm

p. 40, "I didn't back away . . .": Michael R. Lemov, "John Moss and the battle for freedom of information, 41 years later," *Nieman Watchdog*, July 3, 2007. www.niemanwatchdog.org/index.cfm?fuseaction=background. view&backgroundid=00191

p. 41, "Whatever right . . .": Drury, "U.S. Suppression of News Charged."

p. 41, "stated a general principle . . .": Allen Drury, "Government Attacked on Information Policy," *New York Times*, November 13, 1955, E6.

p. 42, "The present trend . . .": Thomas, "John E. Moss, 84, Is Dead; Father of Anti-Secrecy Law."

p. 46, "clearly unwarranted withholdings . . .": Thomas C. Hennings, Subcommittee on Constitutional Rights hearings, Cong. Record, 85th Congress, Senate, 1st session, May 23, 1957, 6683–6684.

p. 47, "paper curtain.": *New York Times*, "2 Bid Congress End the 'Paper Curtain,'" February 8, 1958, 17.

p. 47, "President Eisenhower signed . . .": Associated Press, "Eisenhower Signs Information Bill," *New York Times*, August 13, 1958, 15.

p. 47, "Moss himself . . .": John E. Moss, "Anti-Secrecy Law Is Hailed by Moss," *New York Times*, August 17, 1958, 66.

Chapter Three

p. 49, "By 1958 . . .": United Press International, "Pentagon Removes Secrecy Designation from 650 Million Pages of Pre-'46 Data," *New York Times*, October 4, 1958, 8.

p. 51, "The press regards . . .": Department of Defense, Committee on Classified Information, "Report to the Secretary of Defense by the Committee on Classified Information," Washington: Department of Defense, November 8, 1956, 6.

p. 51, "Being a democracy . . .": "Report to the Secretary of Defense by the Committee on Classified Information," 1.

p. 52, "a vast, intricate . . .": "Appendix A: 8. A Culture of Secrecy," *Report of the Commission on Protecting and Reducing Government Secrecy: 1997*, Senate Document 105-2, 103rd Cong., Washington, DC: U.S. Government Printing Office, 1997, www.fas.org/sgp/library/moynihan/appa8.html

p. 53, "Secrets had become . . .": "Appendix A: 8. A Culture of Secrecy."

p. 55, "It just does not . . .": *Time* magazine, "Science: Prizewinners on Secrecy," June 29, 1959. www.time.com/time/magazine/article/ 0,9171,864695,00.html

p. 56, "rather minimal . . .": "Scientists Detect Harm in Secrecy," *New York Times*, June 15, 1959, 11.

p. 57, "fullest possible freedom . . .": Associated Press, "Johnson Pledges Full Information," *New York Times*, November 19, 1960, 45.

p. 57, "a major improvement . . .": Associated Press, "Program Started to Limit Secrecy," *Tuscaloosa News*, September 22, 1961, 3.

p. 58, "no major change . . .": Austin C. Wehrwein, "Secrecy Report Scores Kennedy," *New York Times*, November 10, 1962, 52.

p. 58, "brilliantly controlled . . .": Laurence Chang and Peter Kornbluh, eds., *The Cuban Missile Crisis, 1962*, 2nd edition, New York: The New Press, 1998. www.gwu.edu/~nsarchiv/nsa/cuba_mis_cri/declass.htm

p. 60, "A government can . . .": John H. Kessel, "Mr. Kennedy and the Manufacture of News," *Parliamentary Affairs*, 1963, XVI: 293-301.

p. 60, "Two top-ranking . . .": Cabell Phillips, "2 U.S. Aides Back Secrecy in Crisis," *New York Times*, March 26, 1963, 1.

p. 61, "as is possible . . .": United Press International, "U.S. Assures Panel on Vietnam News," *New York Times*, May 26, 1963, 1.

p. 61, "Instead of hiding . . .": United Press International, "U.S. News Policy on Saigon Is IIit," *New York Times*, October 1, 1963, 8.

p. 62, "too much . . .": United Press International, "Freedom-Of-Information Bill Hearings To Open," *St. Petersburg Times*, October 28, 1963, 6A.

p. 62, "We should not kid . . .": Associated Press, "Rep. Moss Continues War on Secrecy," *Palm Beach Post*, May 3, 1964, A8.

p. 63, "the lowest ebb . . .": Associated Press, "Press Group Says U.S. News Freedom Is at 'Lowest Ebb,'" *New York Times*, October 28, 1963, 7.

p. 64, "The negotiations . . .": George Kennedy, "Freedom of Information: How Americans got their right to know," American Society of Newspaper Editors, 1996, www.johnemossfoundation.org/foi/kennedy.htm

p. 64, "I did what . . .": Michael R. Lemov, "John Moss and the battle for freedom of information, 41 years later," *Nieman Watchdog*, July 3, 2007. www.niemanwatchdog.org/index.cfm?fuseaction=background.view&backgroundid=00191

p. 65, "In defense, . . .": Associated Press, "Rep. Moss Continues War on Secrecy," *Palm Beach Post*, May 3, 1964, A8.

p. 67, "I will not . . .": Harry Kelly, "Drive Against Secrecy Stalls," Associated Press, *Free Lance-Star*, August 9, 1965, 6.

pp. 67–68, "Although the theory . . .": Associated Press, "An Information Bill Is Passed by Senate," *New York Times*, October 14, 1965, 36.

p. 68, "The unanimous action . . .": Charles Nicodemus, "House Shoo-In: 'Freedom of Information' Bill," *Chicago Daily News*, June 10, 1966, www.gwu.edu/~nsarchiv/NSAEBB/NSAEBB194/Document%209.pdf

p. 69, "Moss, explaining . . .": Nicodemus, "House Shoo-In: 'Freedom of Information' Bill."

p. 70, "With the continuing . . .": Nicodemus, "House Shoo-In: 'Freedom of

Information' Bill.'"

p. 70, "Freedom of speech...": "People's Right to Know at Stake," *Los Angeles Times*, June 17, 1966, http://www.gwu.edu/~nsarchiv/NSAEBB/NSAEBB194/Document%209.pdf

p. 70, "the right of a free...": Beckler and Price, "Fight Against Secrecy Nears End."

pp. 70–71, "He hated...": Bill Moyers, "Politics and Economy: Bill Moyers on the Freedom of Information Act," *Bill Moyers' Journal*, PBS, April 5, 2002. www.pbs.org/now/commentary/moyers4.html

p. 71, "In his statement...": Lyndon B. Johnson, "Statement by the President Upon Signing S. 1160," San Antonio, TX: Office of the White House Press Secretary: July 4, 1966. www.gwu.edu/~nsarchiv/NSAEBB/NSAEBB194/Document%2037.pdf

p. 72, "For the first time...": Beckler and Price, "Fight Against Secrecy Nears End."

p. 72, "It is this device...": Blair, "Information Bill Sent to Johnson."

Chapter Four

p. 75, "Information, particularly...": Walter Rugaber, "Consumers Press Drive to Tap Big Reservoir of Federal Data," *New York Times*, September 2, 1969, 24.

p. 75, "The press...": Rugaber, "Consumers Press Drive to Tap Big Reservoir of Federal Data."

p. 76, "Vast amounts...": George Kennedy, "Freedom of Information: How Americans got their right to know," American Society of Newspaper Editors, 1996. www.johnemossfoundation.org/foi/kennedy.htm

p. 78, "An editorial in *Time*...": Editorial, "The People's Right to Know: How Much or How Little?" *Time* magazine, January 11, 1971, www.time.com/time/magazine/article/0,9171,876841,00.html

pp. 79–80, "As a report...": Senate Subcommittee on Administrative Practice and Procedure, "Freedom of Information Act Source Book: Legislative Materials, Cases, Articles," Washington, DC: U.S. Government Printing Office, 1974, 1. www.llsdc.org/attachments/files/184/FOIA-LH.pdf

p. 84, "The expectation...": Senate Subcommittee on Administrative Practice and Procedure, "Freedom of Information Act Source Book: Legislative Materials, Cases, Articles," Washington, DC: U.S. Government Printing Office, 1974, iii, www.llsdc.org/attachments/files/184/FOIA-LH.pdf

p. 84, "This bill...": Richard L. Madden, "By 383 to 8, House Votes Bill to Strengthen Public's Access to Government Information and Records," *New York Times*, March 15, 1974.

p. 84, "We have seen...": Richard L. Madden, "Senate Votes Bill to Ease Access to Federal Documents," *New York Times*, May 31, 1974.

pp. 84–85, "I reviewed . . .": Howard H. Baker Jr., 120 Cong. Rec. 36, 874, cited in "Ready . . . Aim . . . FOIA! A Survey of the Freedom of Information Act in Post 9/11 U.S.," by Ava Barbour, *Public Interest Law Journal*, 13:2, September 3, 2004, 215.

p. 87, "Let our voices . . .": James M. Naughton, "House Overrides Two Ford Vetoes by Huge Margins," *New York Times*, November 21, 1974, 1.

p. 87, "Hasn't the White House . . .": Naughton, "House Overrides Two Ford Vetoes by Huge Margins."

p. 87, "Two recent tragedies . . .": Associated Press, "Senate Defeats 2 Ford Vetoes, Matching House Action on Bills," *New York Times*, November 22, 1974, 21.

p. 91, "Congress's findings . . .": "Text of Senate FOIA Amendment Bills," S. 1939 (proposed legislation), *FOIA Update*, 12:4, 1991, 2. www.justice.gov/oip/foia_updates/Vol_XII_4/page2.htm

p. 92, "Since 1966 . . .": William Clinton, speech on signing the 1996 FOIA amendments into law, October 2, 1996. www.justice.gov/oip/foia_updates/Vol_XVII_4/page2.htm

Chapter Five

p. 95, "Public scrutiny . . .": Patrick Leahy, Charles Grassley, and Arlen Specter, "Interim Report on FBI Oversight in the 107th Congress by the Senate Judiciary Committee: FISA Implementation Failures," February 2003. www.fas.org/irp/congress/2003_rpt/fisa.html

p. 95, "We must continue . . .": Russell Feingold, "On Opposing the U.S.A. Patriot Act," address given to the Associated Press Managing Editors Conference, Milwaukee, WI: October 12, 2001. www.archipelago.org/vol6-2/feingold.htm

p. 95, "a sea change . . .": Adam Clymer, "Government Openness at Issue As Bush Holds On to Records," *New York Times*, January 3, 2003, A1.

p. 96, "Ashcroft issued a memorandum . . .": John Ashcroft, internal memorandum, October 12, 2001, published as "The Ashcroft Memo," Arlington, VA: Coalition of Journalists for Open Government, 2005-2008. www.cjog.org/back ground_the_ashcroft_memo.html

p. 97, "the fear of God . . .": Ellen Nakashima, "Bush View of Secrecy Is Stirring Frustration," *Washington Post*, March 3, 2002, A4.

p. 98, "Keeping us . . .": Moyers, "Politics and Economy: Bill Moyers on the Freedom of Information Act," *Bill Moyers' Journal*, PBS, April 5, 2002, www.pbs.org/now/commentary/moyers4.html

p. 99, "undercuts the public's . . .": Adam Clymer, "House Panel Seeks Release of Presidential Papers," *New York Times*, October 10, 2002, A32.

p. 99, "I believe . . .": Bill Moyers, "Secret Government," *Bill Moyers' Journal*, PBS, April 5, 2002. www.pbs.org/now/transcript/transcript_secret gov.html

p. 99, "more interested in creating a new policy . . .": Neil A. Lewis, "Bush Claims Executive Privilege in Response to House Inquiry," *New York Times*, December 14, 2001, A26.

p. 100, "What rationale . . .": Thomas Mitchell, "'Knowledge will forever govern ignorance,'" *Las Vegas Review-Journal*, August 26, 2007. www.lvrj.com/opinion/9380501.html

p. 101, "done a serious . . .": Howard F. Jaeckel, Letter to the Editor, *New York Times*, July 4, 2006.

p. 101, "I don't know . . .": Frank Rich, "Can't Win the War? Bomb the Press!" *New York Times*, July 2, 2006, http://select.nytimes.com/2006/07/02/opinion/02rich.html?scp=1&sq=%22Can%27t+Win+the+War%3F+Bomb+the+Press%21%22&st=nyt

p. 102, "never known . . .": Adam Clymer, "Government Openness at Issue As Bush Holds On to Records," *New York Times*, January 3, 2003, A1.

p. 105, "By trying . . .": Elizabeth Williamson, "White House Secrecy Starts to Give," *Washington Post*, January 13, 2008. www.washingtonpost.com/wp-dyn/content/article/2008/01/12/AR2008011202308_2.html

p. 108, "Secrecy and . . .": Ellis Rubinstein, "Editorial," *Science*, 270: 5239, November 17, 1995, 1099.

p. 108, "Restrictions on access . . .": Federation of American Scientists, *2007 Annual Report*, Washington, DC, 2007, 8.

p. 108, "Valuable resources . . .": House Subcommittee on Government Management, Information and Technology, "Statement of Dr. Bruce Alberts before the Subcommittee," 106th Congress, 1st session, July 15, 1999. http://www7.nationalacademies.org/ocga/testimony/foia.asp

p. 110, "free access . . .": "The Freedom of the Press Act," Sveriges Riksdag, www.riksdagen.se/templates/R_Page___8908.aspx

p. 111, "The culture . . .": David Banisar, "Freedom of Information Around the World 2006: A Global Survey of Access to Government Records Laws," Privacy International, July 4, 2006, 57–58, 63, 70, 141. http://freedominfo.org/documents/global_survey2006.pdf

pp. 113–114, "The constitutional health . . .": Emily Berman, "Executive Privilege: A Legislative Remedy," Brennan Center for Justice, New York: New York University School of Law: June 21, 2009. www.brennancenter.org/content/resource/executive_privilege_a_legislative_remedy/

p. 114, "The public is only . . .": Banisar, "Freedom of Information Around the World 2006," 6.

p. 114, "helps us . . .": Ellen Smith, "Assault on Freedom of Information: The Public Has a Right to Know how Decisions Are Made," *Mine Safety and Health News*, July 15, 2004.

p. 114, "The Freedom . . .": Barack Obama, "Remarks by the President in Welcoming Senior Staff and Cabinet Secretaries to the White House,"

Washington, DC: White House Press Office, January 21, 2009. www.whitehouse.gov/the_press_office/RemarksofthePresidentinWelcomingSeniorStaffandCabinetSecretariestotheWhiteHouse

pp. 115–116, "For a long time . . .": Obama, "Remarks by the President."

p. 117, "they are afraid . . .": Carol D. Leonnig, "More than 300 public-records lawsuits filed in Obama's first year," *Washington Post*, January 27, 2010. www.washingtonpost.com/wp-dyn/content/article/2010/01/26/AR2010012602048.html

p. 117, "The Justice Department . . .": Jake Tapper, "Obama Administration Maintains Bush Position on 'Extraordinary Rendition' Lawsuit," ABC News, February 9, 2009. http://blogs.abcnews.com/politicalpunch/2009/02/obama-administr.html

p. 117, "[Attorney General] . . .": Tapper, "Obama Administration Maintains Bush Position on 'Extraordinary Rendition' Lawsuit."

p. 118, "Based on . . .": Michael D. Shear, "Government openness is tested by Salahi case," *Washington Post*, December 4, 2009.

p. 118, "It doesn't even . . .": Shear, "Government openness is tested by Salahi case."

p. 118, "The Obama administration . . .": "Sunshine and Shadows: The Clear Obama Message for Freedom of Information Meets Mixed Results," National Security Archive, March 16, 2010. www.gwu.edu/~nsarchiv/NSAEBB/NSAEBB308/index.htm

pp. 118–119, "The government should not . . .": John E. Moss, "What You Don't Know Will Hurt You," *University of Arizona Bulletin*, 30:4, July 1959. www.johnemossfoundation.org/foi/zengersp.htm

p. 119, "It's always . . .": Bill Moyers, "Politics and Economy: Bill Moyers on the Freedom of Information Act," *Bill Moyers' Journal*, PBS, April 5, 2002, www.pbs.org/now/commentary/moyers4.html

From Bill to Law

pp. 120–123, Senate workload, 1947–2000, www.congresslink.org/print_basics_histmats_workloadstats.htm; House workload, 1947–2000, www.congresslink.org/print_basics_histmats_workloadstats; and Charles W. Johnson, "How Our Laws Are Made," Washington, DC: U.S. Government Printing Office, 1998.

All websites accessible as of September 7, 2010.

Further Information

AUDIO/VIDEO

The Legislative Branch (United States Government). Video, Schlessinger Media, 2002.

BOOKS

Banks, Joan. *The U.S. Constitution. Your Government: How It Works.* Broomall, PA: Chelsea House Publications, 2001.

Barber, Benjamin R. *A Passion for Democracy.* Princeton, NJ: Princeton University Press, 2000.

Hamilton, Lee H. *How Congress Works and Why You Should Care.* Bloomington: Indiana University Press, 2004.

Hudson, David L. Jr. *Open Government: An American Tradition Faces National Security, Privacy, and Other Challenges.* New York: Facts on File, 2005.

Weiss, Ann E. *Who's to Know?: Information, the Media, and Public Awareness.* Boston: Houghton Mifflin Harcourt, 1990.

WEBSITES

Brennan Center for Justice
www.brennancenter.org

DATA.gov: Access to government data via the Internet
www.data.gov/

Federation of American Scientists Project on Government Secrecy
www.fas.org/programs/ssp/govsec/index.html

First Amendment Center
www.firstamendmentcenter.org

Freedom of Information Center, University of Missouri
www.nfoic.org/foi-center

James Madison Project
www.jamesmadisonproject.org

John E. Moss Foundation
www.johnemossfoundation.org

Marion Brechner Citizen Access Project, College of Journalism and Communications, University of Florida
www.citizenaccess.org

National Archives and Records Administration's Freedom of Information Act
www.archives.gov/foia

National Security Archive
www.gwu.edu/~nsarchiv/index.html

Open Society Institute & Soros Foundations Network
www.soros.org

President Obama's Open Government Initiative
www.whitehouse.gov/open

Public Citizen
www.citizen.org

Reporters Committee for Freedom of the Press
www.rcfp.org

U.S. Department of Justice: Freedom of Information Act
www.justice.gov/oip

Western Organization of Resource Councils Guide to Using the FOIA
www.worc.org/userfiles/Use-the-FOIA.pdf

Bibliography

ARTICLES

Adams, John. "A Dissertation on the Canon and Feudal Law," 1765. By Teaching American History.org. Ashland, OH: Ashbrook Center for Public Affairs, Ashland University, 2006–2008.

American President: An Online Reference Resource: *George Washington*, Charlottesville, VA: Miller Center of Public Affairs, University of Virginia, 2010. http://millercenter.org/

"America's First Newspaper." Archiving Early America. www.earlyamerica. com/earlyamerica/firsts/newspaper

Arango, Tim. "Despite Budgets, Some Newsrooms Persist in costly Fight for Records." *New York Times*, February 14, 2010, B1.

Arnold, Martin. "Ford Vetoes Effort to Improve Access to Government Data." *New York Times*, October 18, 1974, 16.

Arnow, Pat. "From Self-Censorship to Official Censorship." *FAIR: Fairness & Accuracy In Reporting*, March/April 2007.

Associated Press. "Eisenhower Signs Information Bill." *New York Times*, August 13, 1958, 15.

——. "House Panel Urges Curbs on U.S. Secrecy Practices." *New York Times*, May 25, 1973, 12.

——. "An Information Bill Is Passed by Senate." *New York Times*, October 14, 1965, 36.

——. "Johnson Pledges Full Information." *New York Times*, November 19, 1960, 45.

——. "News Managing Laid to Kennedy." *New York Times*, February 25, 1963, 5.

——. "Newsmen Accuse Administration of Attempt to Impose Secrecy." *New York Times*, November 1, 1965, 24.

——. "Press Group Says U.S. News Freedom Is at 'Lowest Ebb.'" *New York Times*, October 28, 1963, 7.

——. "Program Started to Limit Secrecy." *Tuscaloosa News*, September 22, 1961, 3.

——. "Rep. Moss Continues War on Secrecy." *Palm Beach Post*, May 3, 1964, A8.

——. "Secrecy on Army Report Questioned." *Lewiston Daily Sun*, September 25, 1962, 6.

——. "Senate Defeats 2 Ford Vetoes, Matching House Action on Bills." *New York Times*, November 22, 1974, 21.

——. "Tenn. Plant's Nuclear Woes Kept Secret." *Richmond Times-Dispatch*, August 21, 2007, A4.

Banisar, David. "Freedom of Information Around the World 2006: A Global

Survey of Access to Government Records Laws." Privacy International, July 4, 2006.

Barbour, Ava. "Ready . . . Aim . . . FOIA! A Survey of the Freedom of Information Act in Post 9/11 U.S." *Public Interest Law Journal*, 13:2, September 3, 2004.

Beckler, John W., and Bem Price. "Fight Against Secrecy Nears End." *Arizona Republic*, June 12, 1966, 16B.

Berman, Emily. "Executive Privilege: A Legislative Remedy." Brennan Center for Justice. New York: New York University School of Law, June 21, 2009. www.brennancenter.org/

Blair, William M. "Information Bill Sent to Johnson." *New York Times*, June 21, 1966, 21.

Carr, David. "The Media Equation: Let the Sun Shine." *New York Times*, July 23, 2007.

Chaffin, G. S. Letter to the Editor. *New York Times*, July 4, 2006.

Clymer, Adam. "Government Openness at Issue As Bush Holds On to Records." *New York Times*, January 3, 2003, A1.

Department of Justice. "DOJ FOIA and Privacy Act Regulations," 2009. www. justice.gov/oip/04 1 1.html

——. "Government Adopts New Standard for Openness." Press release, October 4, 1993. www.fas.org/sgp/clinton/reno.html

Doyle, Michael. "Right-to-know crusader Moss was FBI's thorn." *Sacramento Bee*, September 2, 2001.

Drury, Allen. "Government Attacked on Information Policy." *New York Times*, November 13, 1955, E6.

——. "Newsmen Testify at Senate Inquiry." *New York Times*, January 5, 1956, 1.

——. "U.S. Suppression of News Charged." *New York Times*, November 8, 1955, 25.

Editorial. "The People's Right to Know: How Much or How Little?" *Time* magazine, January 11, 1971.

Editorial. "Secret Dangers; Sealing Records About Hazardous Operations Can Threaten Public Safety." *Columbus Dispatch*, August 27, 2007, 6A.

Feingold, Russell. "On Opposing the U.S.A. Patriot Act." Address given to the Associated Press Managing Editors Conference, Milwaukee, WI: October 12, 2001.

"Frequent Filers: Businesses Make FOIA Their Business." Coalition of Journalists for Open Government. Arlington, VA, July 3, 2006.

Green, Sterling F. "Secrecy Abuses Up Under Ike, Harry: ACLU." Associated Press, *St. Petersburg Times*, November 4, 1955, 2.

Grimaldi, James V. "National Zoo Cites Privacy Concerns in its Refusal to Release Animal's Medical Records." *Washington Post*, May 6, 2002, E12.

Haywood, O. G. Jr. "Note to Dr. Fidler from O. G. Haywood, Jr. on Medical Experiments on Humans, April 17, 1947." Department of Energy.

Hodes, Scott A. "FOIA Facts: Ronald Reagan's FOIA Legacy." *LLRX: Law and Technology Resources for Legal Professionals*, June 21, 2004.

Holliday, Taylor. "How to File an FOIA Request." First Amendment Center. www.firstamendmentcenter.org/

House workload, 1947–2000. www.congresslink.org/

Jaeckel, Howard F. Letter to the Editor. *New York Times*, July 4, 2006.

Kaufman, Michael T. "Melvin Barnet, 83, Times Editor Fired After Charge of Communism." *New York Times*, June 19, 1998, B11.

Kelly, Harry. "Drive Against Secrecy Stalls." *Free Lance-Star*, August 9, 1965, 6.

Kennedy, George. "Freedom of Information: How Americans got their right to know," American Society of Newspaper Editors, 1996, www.johnemoss foundation.org/

Kessel, John H. "Mr. Kennedy and the Manufacture of News." *Parliamentary Affairs*, 1963, XVI: 293–301.

Lemov, Michael R. "John Moss and the battle for freedom of information, 41 years later." *Nieman Watchdog*, July 3, 2007.

Leonnig, Carol D. "More than 300 public-records lawsuits filed in Obama's first year." *Washington Post*, January 27, 2010.

Lewis, Neil A. "Bush Claims Executive Privilege in Response to House Inquiry." *New York Times*, December 14, 2001, A26.

Loftus, Joseph A. "Censorship Code for War Shaped." *New York Times*, June 8, 1963, 9.

Madden, Richard L. "By 383 to 8, House Votes Bill to Strengthen Public's Access to Government Information and Records." *New York Times*, March 15, 1974.

———. "Senate Votes Bill to Ease Access to Federal Documents." *New York Times*, May 31, 1974.

Madison, James. Letter, August 4, 1822. http://memory.loc.gov/

Mitchell, Thomas. "'Knowledge will forever govern ignorance.'" *Las Vegas Review-Journal*, August 26, 2007.

Moss, John E. "Anti-Secrecy Law Is Hailed by Moss." *New York Times*, August 17, 1958, 66.

———. "What You Don't Know Will Hurt You." *University of Arizona Bulletin*, 30:4, July 1959.

Moyers, Bill. "Bill Moyers Interviews Chuck Lewis." *Bill Moyers' Journal*. PBS, February 7, 2003.

———. "Politics and Economy: Bill Moyers on the Freedom of Information Act." *Bill Moyers' Journal*. PBS, April 5, 2002.

———. "Politics & Economy: Veil of Secrecy." *Bill Moyers' Journal*. PBS, December 12, 2003.

———. "Secret Government." *Bill Moyers' Journal*. PBS. April 5, 2002.

Nakashima, Ellen. "Bush View of Secrecy Is Stirring Frustration." *Washington Post*, March 3, 2002, A4.

Naughton, James M. "Agnew Quits Vice Presidency and Admits Tax Evasion in '67." *New York Times*, October 11, 1973, 1.

———. "House Overrides Two Ford Vetoes by Huge Margins." *New York Times*, November 21, 1974, 1.

———. "The Eastland Inquiry." January 8, 1956, E1.

———. "President Eisenhower's Week—Six Highlights in Washington and on His New England Trip." July 3, 1955, E1.

———. "Scientists Detect Harm in Secrecy." June 15, 1959, 11.

———. "Summary of Report Criticizing Secrecy." November 4, 1955, 11.

——. "2 Bid Congress End the 'Paper Curtain.'" February 8, 1958, 17.

Nicodemus, Charles. "House Shoo-In: 'Freedom of Information' Bill." *Chicago Daily News*, June 10, 1966.

"People's Right to Know at Stake." *Los Angeles Times*, June 17, 1966.

Phillips, Cabell. "2 U.S. Aides Back Secrecy in Crisis." *New York Times*, March 26, 1963, 1.

Porter, Russell. "Freer News Flow With Kennedy Is Forecast to Sigma Delta Chi." *New York Times*, December 2, 1960, 15.

"The Press: *Eastland* v. *the Times*." *Time* magazine, January 16, 1956.

Relyea, Harold C. "Access to Government Information in the United States." *CRS Report for Congress*, January 7, 2005.

——. "Freedom of information and the right to know: the origins and applications of the Freedom of Information Act." *The Journal of Academic Librarianship*, 27: 1, January 2001, 59–60.

Reston, James. "Security vs. Freedom: An Analysis of the Controversy Stirred by Recommendation to Curb Information." *New York Times*, June 25, 1957, 17.

Rich, Frank. "Can't Win the War? Bomb the Press!" *New York Times*, July 2, 2006.

Rosen, Ruth. "On the Public's Right to Know: The Day Ashcroft Censored Freedom of Information." *San Francisco Chronicle*, January 6, 2002, D4.

Rubinstein, Ellis. "Editorial." *Science*, 270:5239, November 17, 1995, 1099.

Rugaber, Walter. "Consumers Press Drive to Tap Big Reservoir of Federal Data." *New York Times*, September 2, 1969, 24.

Sasser, Charles W. "Cold War: Bay of Pigs Invasion." *Modern Warfare*, November 1989.

"Science: Prizewinners on Secrecy." *Time* magazine, June 29, 1959.

Senate workload, 1947–2000. www.congresslink.org/

Shane, Scott. "A.C.L.U. Lawyers Mine Documents for Truth." *New York Times*, August 29, 2009, A4.

Shane, Scott, Mark Mazzetti, and Helene Cooper. "Obama Reverses Key Bush Security Policies." *New York Times*, January 23, 2009, A16.

Sinclair, Ward. "The Man Who Perfected Oversight." *Washington Post*, January 14, 1979.

Smith, Ellen. "Assault on Freedom of Information." *Mine Safety and Health News*, July 15, 2004.

"Text of Senate FOIA Amendment Bills." S. 1939 (proposed legislation). *FOIA Update*, 12:4, 1991, 2.

Thomas, Robert McG. Jr., "John E. Moss, 84, Is Dead; Father of Anti-Secrecy Law." *New York Times*, December 6, 1997, D15.

Toth, Robert C. "Federal Leaders Accused on News." *New York Times*, March 20, 1963, 1.

Trussell, C. P. "House Votes Curb on Use of Secrecy." *New York Times*, April 17, 1958, 17.

United Press International. "Freedom-Of-Information Bill Hearings To Open." *St. Petersburg Times*, October 28, 1963, 6A.

———. "Hennings Critical of Executive Rights." *New York Times*, August 2, 1958, 44.

———. "House Unit Passes Information Bill." *New York Times*, March 31, 1966, 42.

———. "Pentagon Removes Secrecy Designation from 650 Million Pages of Pre-'46 Data." *New York Times*, October 4, 1958, 8.

———. "President Backs Air Force Secrecy on Missile Report." *New York Times*, November 13, 1958, 1.

———. "U.S. Assures Panel on Vietnam News." *New York Times*, May 26, 1963, 1.

———. "U.S. News Policy on Saigon Is Hit." *New York Times*, October 1, 1963, 8.

vanden Heuvel, Katrina. "Nation and NY Times: Bay of Pigs Déjà vu." *The Nation*, July 6, 2006.

"Watkins Aftermath." *New York Times*, July 14, 1957, 136.

Weart, William G. "Official Secrecy Called Perilous." *New York Times*, November 24, 1957, 54.

Weaver, Warren Jr. "At Home: The President's Popularity Seems to Be Slipping." *New York Times*, July 7, 1963, E3.

Wehrwein, Austin C. "Bill Is Proposed on Data Secrecy." *New York Times*, September 16, 1960, 1.

———. "Secrecy Report Scores Kennedy." *New York Times*, November 10, 1962, 52.

Williamson, Elizabeth. "White House Secrecy Starts to Give." *Washington Post*, January 13, 2008.

"Wilson Revamps Labeling of Data." *New York Times*, July 20, 1957, 6.

BOOKS/BOOKLETS

Andrew, Christopher. *For the President's Eyes Only: Secret Intelligence and the American Presidency from Washington to Bush*. New York: Harper Perennial, 1996.

Bok, Sissela. *Secrets*. New York: Vintage Books, 1989.

Casey, William L. Jr., John E. Marthinsen, and Laurence S. Moss. *Entrepreneurship, Productivity, and the Freedom of Information Act*. Lexington, MA: Lexington Books, 1983.

Chang, Laurence, and Peter Kornbluh, eds. *The Cuban Missile Crisis, 1962*, 2nd edition. New York: The New Press, 1998.

Cobb, Stephen. *Privacy for Business: Web Sites and Email*. St. Augustine, FL: Dreva Hill LLC, 2002.

Cross, Harold. *The People's Right to Know*. New York: Columbia University Press, 1953.

Edel, Wilbur. *Kekionga!: The Worst Defeat in the History of the U.S. Army*. Westport, CT: Praeger Publishers, 1997.

Henry, William Wirt. *Patrick Henry: Life, Correspondence and Speeches*, vol. 3. New York: Charles Scribner's Sons, 1891.

Leslie, Gregg, and Corinna Zarek, eds. *Open Government Guide*, 5th edition. Arlington, VA: The Reporters Committee for Freedom of the Press, 2006.

Johnson, Charles W. "How Our Laws Are Made." Washington, DC: U.S. Government Printing Office, 1998.

Moynihan, Daniel Patrick. *Secrecy: The American Experience.* New Haven: Yale University Press, 1998.

O'Brien, David M. *The Public's Right to Know: The Supreme Court and the First Amendment.* New York: Praeger Publishers, 1981.

Pratte, Paul Alfred. *Gods Within the Machine: A History of the American Society of Newspapers.* Westport, CT: Praeger Publishers, 1995.

Steinberg, Charles S. *The Information Establishment: Our Government and the Media.* New York: Hastings House, Publishers, 1980.

Wasby, Stephen L. *Civil Liberties: Policy and Policy Making.* Edison, NJ: Transaction Publishers, 1976.

COURT CASES

Critical Mass Energy Project v. *NRC,* 830 F.2d 278 (D.C. Cir. 1987).

EPA v. *Mink,* 410 U.S. 73 (1973).

New York Times Co. v. *United States,* 403 US 713 (1971).

Watkins v. *United States,* 354 U.S. 178 (1957).

DOCUMENTS, REPORTS, AND LAWS

Administrative Procedure Act (APA), 5 U.S.C.A. §§ 501 et seq.

Ashcroft, John. Internal memorandum, October 12, 2001.

"Clarifying and Protecting the Right of the Public to Information and for Other Purposes." Senate Report No. 1219, 88th Cong., 2nd Session, July 22, 1964.

Clark, Tom C. "Attorney General's Manual on the Administrative Procedure Act, 1947." ABA Administrative Procedure DataBase. www.law.fsu.edu/library/admin/1947ii.html

Clinton, William. Speech on signing the 1996 FOIA amendments into law, October 2, 1996.

Congressional Record. Washington, DC: U.S. Government Printing Office.

Federation of American Scientists. *2007 Annual Report.* Washington, DC, 2007.

Freedom of Information Act, 5 U.S.C. Section 552, as amended by Public Law No. 104-231, 110 Stat. 3048.

"Freedom of Information Act Source Book: Legislative Materials, Cases, Articles." Senate Subcommittee on Administrative Practice and Procedure. Washington, DC: U.S. Government Printing Office, 1974.

"The Freedom of the Press Act." Sveriges Riksdag. www.riksdagen.se/templates/R_Page___8908.aspx

Government in the Sunshine Act, 5 U.S.C., Section 552b.

Johnson, Lyndon B. "Statement by the President Upon Signing S. 1160."

Leahy, Patrick, Charles Grassley, and Arlen Specter. "Interim Report on FBI Oversight in the 107th Congress by the Senate Judiciary Committee: FISA Implementation Failures." February 2003.

Obama, Barack. "Remarks by the President in Welcoming Senior Staff and Cabinet Secretaries to the White House," January 21, 2009.

"Report of the Commission on Protecting and Reducing Government Secrecy:

1997." Senate Document 105-2, 103rd Congress, Washington, DC: U.S. Government Printing Office, 1997.

"Report to the Secretary of Defense by the Committee on Classified Information." Washington, DC: Department of Defense, November 8, 1956.

S. 2488—110th Congress: OPEN Government Act of 2007. GovTrack.us. www.govtrack.us/congress/bill.xpd?bill=s110-2488

WEBSITES

The American Presidency Project
www.presidency.ucsb.edu

The Avalon Project, Documents in Law, History and Diplomacy
http://avalon.law.yale.edu

Database of federal legislation
www.govtrack.us

Federation of American Scientists Project on Government Secrecy
www.fas.org/programs/ssp/govsec/index.html

Freedominfo.org: Global network of freedom of information advocates
http://freedominfo.org

James Madison Project
www.jamesmadisonproject.org

John E. Moss Foundation
www.johnemossfoundation.org

National Archives and Records Administration's Freedom of Information Act
www.archives.gov/foia/

The National Security Archive, George Washington University
www.gwu.edu/~nsarchiv/index.html

Reporters Committee for Freedom of the Press
www.rcfp.org

U.S. Department of Justice, Freedom of Information Act
www.justice.gov/oip/index.html

All websites accessible as of September 7, 2010.

Index

Page numbers in **boldface** are illustrations, tables, and charts.

About the Author

SUSAN DUDLEY GOLD has worked as a reporter for a daily newspaper, managing editor of two statewide business magazines, and freelance writer for several regional publications. She has written more than four dozen books for middle-school and high-school students on a variety of topics, including American history, health issues, law, and space.

Gold has won numerous awards for her work, including most recently the selection of Loving v. Virginia: *Lifting the Ban Against Interracial Marriage*, part of Marshall Cavendish's Supreme Court Milestones series, as one of the Notable Social Studies Trade Books for Young People in 2009. Three other books in that series have received recognition: United States v. Amistad: *Slave Ship Mutiny,* selected as a Carter G. Woodson Honor Book in 2008; and Tinker v. Des Moines: *Free Speech for Students* in 2008 and Roberts v. Jaycees: *Women's Rights* in 2010, both awarded first place in the National Federation of Press Women's communications contest, nonfiction juvenile book category.

Gold has written several titles in the Landmark Legislation series for Marshall Cavendish. She is the author of a number of books on Maine history. She and her husband, John Gold, own and operate a web design and publishing business in Maine. They have one son, Samuel; a granddaughter, Callie; and a grandson, Alexander.